Road Trip

One Doctor's Call to Haiti

James Ingvoldstad

Carpenter's Son Publishing

Road Trip

©2019 by James Ingvoldstad

Published by Carpenter's Son Publishing, Franklin, Tennessee

Published in association with Larry Carpenter of
Christian Book Services, LLC
www.christianbookservices.com

Cover Design by Nelly Sanchez

Interior Design by Suzanne Lawing

Edited by Lee Titus Elliott

Cover Photo by Lee Wilder

Printed in the United States of America

978-1-949572-40-7

DEDICATION

This book is dedicated to all the everyday citizens
of Haiti who give from their hearts.

A portion of the royalties will be donated to
the La Gonave Haiti Partners.

"The place God calls you to is the place where your true
gladness and the world's deep hunger meet."
–Frederick Buechner

ACKNOWLEDGMENTS

I extend my sincerest thanks and appreciation to all my family, friends, classmates, and teachers who have influenced me throughout my life.

I relish all the experiences and camaraderie that my fellow travelers and I shared on our trips to Haiti. Thank you.

I am indebted to Tammy Kling, Tiarra Tomkins, and Larry Carpenter for their expertise and enthusiasm in making this book possible.

I thank my writing group, Kelleen, Resa, Aria, and Jo, for their insights and suggestions.

Thank you to La Gonave Haiti Partners and Childspring International. You are the best 501(c) 3s, I know. You provided a solid bridge between the U.S. and Haiti.

Kudos to the members of Covenant Presbyterian Church in Atlanta who embraced the partnership with Nan Mango and other projects on La Gonave.

Finally, I am enormously grateful for my wife Jan, who whole-heartedly supported me with technical advice, enthusiasm, and patience. She kept me on track.

Contents

INTRODUCTION

Over the past four decades of practicing medicine, nothing affected me as much as my trips to Haiti. During the last two decades, I have traveled there enough times to see a different side of the Haitian people than what's sometimes portrayed in the news and media. Simply put, going to Haiti changed my life. It wasn't just about the babies I delivered or the people whom I treated for illness and thanked me. Rather, it was about the overall experiences that I had there. I went to Haiti, thinking I was going to help the underprivileged. I was driven by an altruistic need to serve others. I wanted to make a difference. In reality, many times that was flipped. Unexpectedly, they helped, taught, and influenced me.

The difference that Haitian patients, friends, and strangers made in my life started a ripple effect. First, I had to reevaluate my own priorities and sense of purpose. I had to trust strangers. I had to peel away layers of personal protection that I had constructed over the years. I had to look inward and be honest about what I might find. Then, as I shared stories of my experiences, I encouraged other doctors, nurses, radiology technicians, and members of my church to serve as well. I learned that there was an organization named La Gonave Haiti Partners, which, in coordination with the Episcopal Diocese of Haiti, brought people from different states, church denominations, and civic groups together to assist local villages in projects for clean water, education, agriculture, and animal husbandry, as well as the medical clinics. Our church became involved with them.

Most everyone who went on a trip observed the same abundance of joy that the Haitians had, in spite of all the things they lacked. On every trip, someone would say, "I want some of that joy." And this question would always come up: Are their joy and poverty related? That, I think, is a false correlation. Part of their joy comes from living in the moment and in community. They share, they play, they work, and they dream about a better future.

One of the things we always had to remind ourselves was that we were guests in their country and needed to be sensitive to their culture. We were there to listen and partner with projects that met their needs. Our church had partnered with Nan Mango, a rural community, for several years and had helped them build a church, a cistern, a latrine, and additional schoolrooms. On one of our trips after new school supplies had been distributed and a new lunch program had been instituted which, for some children, would be their only meal, the lay leaders of our group and their community leaders gathered to discuss future plans. I had worked all day at the clinic, and at dinner we shared our stories. Debbie and Lee, seasoned leaders of many trips, told me that the councilmen discussed a potential irrigation project, a mobile medical clinic, and other community-related efforts. As they were about to end the meeting, a woman in her sixties from the back of the room raised her hand. She spoke up and said, "You have done all these amazing things for us and our children, but we [she pointed to several other women around her] would like to learn how to read." From that woman's dream, the establishment of an adult literacy program became the number one priority.

The people of Haiti desire the same things as we do: better homes, better education, better health. They know the value of relationships as the key to a better life. They have built their lives on community and people, versus money and power. When cell phones became available, it enhanced rather than hindered their sense of community.

Do you want to change your life? Do you want to find out whom you really are? You have to take a chance.

You may not be sure why or where you want to serve. But take that chance. It is a risk that allows you to make an impact and to discover your purpose.

Are you ready?

What follows is a narrative that explores some of these questions.

CHAPTER 1

Road Trip

Sitting in a leather chair that was soft and wrinkled from years of use in my fraternity's cozy library with its sunken slate floor, stained glass windows, and arched ceiling, I felt a sense of comfort and belonging, even though I was just a freshman pledge. The library was not just for reading and philosophical discussions. It had two sturdy tables that were perfect for study—or card games. Friday classes were over, and I was awaiting the arrival of fellow pledge brothers for a game of bridge before dinner. I thought it would just be a normal Friday night.

Soon, I saw one of the "actives" lean up against the doorframe. Wearing penny loafers, wheat jeans, and a long-sleeved blue oxford shirt with cuffs rolled up, he was the epitome of "cool," the status to which I aspired. As I was expecting him to greet me, he simply said two words out loud: "Road trip."

It was the first time I had heard the phrase, but it would not be the last.

His words confounded me. What was he talking about?

Where would we go? Why should we go there? Was I supposed to go? Was I supposed to just suspend my plans and follow this future brother whom I barely knew? Maybe planning and itineraries weren't always necessary. Maybe just going was all that mattered.

Iowa State University, in Ames, Iowa, is located in the middle of America. We had no natural barriers that prevented us from traveling in any direction of the compass, which meant, for me, that we could experience a new adventure at any time. It might be a short trip south to a metropolitan city to catch the first release of a hot new movie or a weekend trip north to aid a small farming community recovering from the ravages of a rogue tornado. Longer school breaks between quarters provided ample opportunity for more adventuresome endeavors, such as teams of two or three brothers studying the freight train schedules so they could ride the rails to New York City and then hitchhike back in a race. The prize? Bragging rights of who got back first or who had the most unique stories.

During Christmas break of our first year in college, one of my best friends from high school and fellow pledge brother and I planned a trip to Los Angeles. His generous uncle in California offered to sell him a 1956 Chevy for one dollar. We just needed to get there. The trip started by riding with a brother headed to his home in Grand Junction, Colorado. Through Nebraska and Colorado we encountered snowstorms and iced roads that required us to use tire chains in the mountain passes. The second leg was a midnight bus ride from Grand Junction to Provo, Utah. Our next plan was to hitchhike, but it seemed like no one was leaving Provo. In desperation, we approached a semi truck driver and asked if we could ride with him. He mumbled something about it being illegal, but he would take us.

He opened the backend of the refrigerated trailer where slabs of beef hung and told us to toss our suitcases on the floor. We climbed in the cab. On the road, his wild antics gave us pause, but we were stuck or committed or stupid. Every car— and especially a Greyhound bus—seemed to be his mortal adversary. As he slowed and enticed them to pass, he'd shout into his rearview mirror, "Come on, puppy dog; I'm gonna blow you off the road." Then, as they approached, a quick dart to the left blocked their advance. When he saw the midnight lights of Las Vegas, he popped some pills and jammed the accelerator. It was full speed ahead. We could only hope that we would survive this final push and that the boldness of our decision would be of some value, besides the Chevy awaiting us. And it was. All that we saw and experienced was worth the adventure. We had stories to tell.

Many years later, after college, medical school, residency training, two years of air force duty, and twenty-two years of private practice, a new adventure called to me. One Saturday morning, a fellow obstetrician-gynecologist and I were operating together. It seemed like any other Saturday morning, until he asked me, "What do you think about the upcoming Haiti trip?"

As I made the incision through the layers of skin, adipose, fascia, and peritoneum, his question went in one ear and out another. As I entered the abdominal cavity, the troublesome fibroid uterus lay deep in the pelvis, waiting to be removed. With our usual precision, we clamped, cut, and sutured the supporting pedicles and vessels that fed the overgrown mass. We were surgeons doing our job. "A chance to cut is a chance to cure" never seemed to be more appropriate. I was focused on doing a good job with the surgery. We successfully removed the diseased organ and began to close.

"What do you think about the Haiti trip?" he asked again.

"What Haiti trip? I have no idea what you're talking about," I replied.

"The one we heard about at Thursday Grand Rounds," he said.

Since I had missed that presentation, I asked him to tell me about it.

"I can't remember her name, but a representative from a global children's organization spoke to us. They identify children in Third World countries who are unable to have complicated surgeries done by doctors in their countries, procure pro bono service from doctors here in the States, and arrange transportation and host families for their stay. She had just returned from La Gonâve in Haiti, where she learned that there was a medical clinic that could benefit from Ob-Gyn services. She hoped some of us might be interested in going there to check it out."

I thought this all sounded very nice. Mission work had been something I had always considered in the back of my mind. Maybe someday, I could obtain more details about the project, check my schedules, and consider some involvement. It seemed like something I could do in the future.

But wait a minute. He had said the "Haiti trip," not the "Haiti project."

"What do you mean the 'Haiti trip'?" I asked.

He replied, "She is returning there next week and is looking for some of us to accompany her and check things out. I can't go."

Again, I was lost in thought. Next week. Really? That's short notice for us planners, for those of us who like to go from A to B to C in a neatly planned line.

We closed the skin. The operation was done. But I could

not stop thinking about my conversation with my colleague. As I stripped off my surgical gown and snapped my gloves into the bucket on the floor, I felt a rumbling from the back of my mind. Exploding out of the deep, repressed archives of the past and overtaking my entire brain came that confounding refrain: "Road trip." That statement, that invitation, that call of the wild that says, "Stop what you are planning. Go to who knows where or why. Go. Just go."

Thus, in March 2001, it began: my road trip to Haiti and all its adventures.

CHAPTER 2

Getting There

The trip had been planned for the week of Easter. I had to make some schedule changes at the office and had to put a long holiday weekend trip to the Florida Gulf Coast on hold. Next, I contacted Sarah, who would be the expedition leader. She explained that this was an exploratory mission to ascertain what infrastructure existed there, what medical services or supplies were needed there, and what we could possibly do in the future. She had recruited two other physicians from another hospital who had already committed to joining the expedition. If I was a surgical case, then I would be classified as an add-on to the schedule. She gave me the flight information and told me to meet them at the airport in three days.

Just like that, I was on my way to Haiti. For the next two days, an uncertain anxiety awakened me at about 4 a.m. every morning. It's that bewitching hour that so often only intensified the ruminations taking over my brain and that offered no solutions to the questions being posed. I did not know any of my traveling companions, nor did I know much about Haiti, except for reports about voodoo, malaria, HIV epidemics, swine flu epidemics, boat people, and other misfortunes. Everything about the trip was cloaked in mystery and uncertainty.

In contrast, the daytime preparations were focused and undisturbed. Obtaining and packing Deet (a potent insect repellant), antibiotics for dysentery and malaria, Advil, proper clothing, a camera, a notebook, and sunscreen were tasks with a beginning and a satisfying end, like mowing the grass or trimming a hedge or removing a diseased organ. Daytime is for accomplishments and surges of adrenaline that cause the heart to beat faster and stronger, the fingers to tingle, and the legs to stride longer and quicker. It was all still under my control. The nighttime brought restless, thrashing, sheet-tossing leg action, palms dripping like a soaker hose, and a pounding heart that threatened to break free from its ribbed cage.

The day of travel finally arrived and brought an end to the ambiguity. Identifying my traveling companions in the swarm of humanity at the airport would require a combination of my innate powers of observation, plus some logic. Since the first leg of our journey took us from Atlanta to Miami, I deemed it best to check in and then go to the departure gate, where there would be fewer passengers to evaluate. Once I got to Gate T-11, it was simple to eliminate the T-shirt-color-coordinated mission groups with sayings like "Give a sole, save a soul," as candidates. It was easy to cast aside the elderly, the men and women dressed in business suits, and the young women dressed for Miss Tropicana auditions, even as it was hard to ignore that last group.

Eventually, I saw two men and a woman wearing closed-toe sandals, cargo pants, and lightweight safari shirts and carrying overloaded backpacks. They seemed to fit the bill. I approached and greeted them. Yes! It was Sarah, Jack, and Howard. A fist pump or a high five seemed like an appropriate congratulatory maneuver, as did sending a freshly exhaled breath onto my right-hand nails and then subtly buffing them on my shirt. My overinflated self-evaluation would not last very long.

Since Sarah had been before, I considered Jack, Howard, and me to be some combination of the Three Musketeers, the Three Amigos, and the Three Stooges.

After saying hello, Sarah asked why I had not been at the check-in counter. They had needed me there in order to assign to my ticket the extra duffle bags of clothes, shoes, pots, pans, and vitamins that were being taken to La Gonâve. I hadn't realized that I was expected to be a Sherpa. My inflated self-image quickly decompressed, and I considered how convenient it would be to slip into one of the briefcases headed to Miami.

Fortunately, Sarah had been able to convince the ticket agent that I had absentmindedly forgotten to rendezvous at check-in but was aware of the contents of the bags. It would not be the last time that the truth would be stretched or the rules bent for a just cause. In fact, I got a minisurge of adrenaline that suggested I was looking forward to being a rebel or a pirate, in addition to being the do-gooder.

Miami International Concourse provided a glimpse of what awaited us in Port-au-Prince. At gate D34, our group of Anglo-Saxon doctors moved to the side while the multitude of Haitians heading home after visiting family or friends in Miami carried shopping bags full of baking supplies or new clothes, shoes, and jeans. As they carried their bags bursting at the seams with goods, they simultaneously balanced new VCRs or stereos on their shoulders. Nearly all the women wore hats and pressed, brightly colored dresses. The men wore suits, ties, and shined shoes. Crowding and funneling their way to the opened boarding door was not forbidden, but expected. It reminded me of ants heading back to the nest after foraging a nearby picnic site. They maintained a dignity within the disorderliness.

I would later learn that Haitians are not as uncomfortable as we are with close body proximity. Where we seem to need a foot of space around us on an elevator, they could easily jam together so one or two more could fit into a space that didn't seem to exist. This cultural difference would become even more evident and, initially, uncomfortable in Port–au-Prince. But we were not there yet.

The two-hour flight to Port-au-Prince was smooth and comfortable. We each enjoyed the traditional snack packet of cheddar cheese, two thin crackers, a thimble-sized box of raisins, and a triangle of Toblerone chocolate. The giant Airbus landed and taxied toward the Toussaint International Terminal, which was named after the leader of the successful slave rebellion that freed the Haitians from the oppressive French rule over two hundred years ago. Finally, our American Airlines plane stopped moving. The exit door was opened, and the steps descending to the tarmac were rolled into place. We were about to enter Haiti.

When we approached the open exit door, we were met with a blast of hot, humid air that carried the scent of charcoal into our nostrils, and we squinted from the brilliant sunlight that highlighted the haze of smoke drifting above the city. At the bottom of our descent, there was no red carpet, as dignitaries would expect. Rather, fifty yards away, by the terminal entry, there stood a small Creole band that consisted of a trumpeter, a guitarist, a keyboardist, and a snare drummer. While they provided us an auditory welcome worthy of any head of state, it also felt as if we could have been on Bourbon Street. I felt in between two different worlds. I tossed two dollars into their tip box.

Once we got inside the terminal and passed through customs, it all changed. The air remained hot and humid, but it had become as still as a rattler preparing to strike. The stirring music of the band was replaced by shouts and animated conversations in Creole as the Haitians once again maneuvered in close proximity to each other, jockeying into position to grab their checked luggage. The odd mixture of sweat, body odor, and counterbalancing perfumes erased the charcoal aroma reminiscent of backyard grilling. At the baggage pickup, the handlers would unload the bags, suitcases, and odd-sized, plastic-wrapped boxes through a double-garage-sized door onto a single conveyor belt. Sometimes, they just threw it all on floor. It was a free for-all. We lacked the skill and initiative to enter the fray, and wondered if our bags would be there once the crowd cleared out. We were, at best, the Three Stooges.

I felt a tap on my right shoulder, turned, and a six-feet-one, 150-pound man stood next to me.

The stranger asked, "Do you need help? Who's your boss man?"

I pointed to Sarah and said, "She is."

The stranger took all the baggage claim slips, enlisted additional help, and gathered our suitcases, bulging duffle bags, and shrink-wrapped pots and pans and loaded them onto trolley carts with expertise.

Next, he asked, "Do you need transportation?"

We told him we had a driver named David waiting.

"Then follow me and stay close. I will take care of you," he replied.

Sure. Trust and skepticism competed for dominance to guide my actions. We could take him up on his offer, or we could choose self-reliance. We chose the former. If he had only said, "Road trip," the decision would have been much easier.

As we exited the terminal, we were confronted with an even more dense and loud mass of humanity. Some tried to grab our bags and carry them for us. Some asked us for money. One young man lifted his T-shirt and showed me a short, plastic catheter tip on his right lower abdomen and uttered the word, "Operation." I could easily tell it was taped to his skin and not coming through it, as he wanted me to believe. I politely refused his request for medical funding. More than once, as I was approached either verbally or physically, I pointed to my new unknown, best friend and said, "Boss man." His presence ended any unsolicited encounters on our way to meeting David with his van.

We at last connected with David. An imposing sight, David had a chest as thick as a whiskey barrel and an abdominal girth to match. The corners of his smile lifted his chipmunk cheeks upward, causing a squint of his eyes that could not obliterate the gleam that resided there. Ropelike muscles that easily tossed the fifty-to-seventy pound bags into and on top of the van defined his forearms. He did not sweat. This was our new boss man. We loaded ourselves into the van and took the ten-minute trip to the adjacent terminal that served multiple small Caribbean airlines and private planes.

Captain Will, an American who ran one of the private island services, was there to greet us and fly us across the bay to La Gonâve. The single-engine plane had a weight restriction. Everything that was being loaded on board must be weighed and evenly distributed in order to maintain proper balance. That included us. Stepping on a scale and seeing your weight displayed on a large circular face—like a hallway grandfather clock—for everyone to see was not expected. Like all first time travelers, in a vain attempt to avoid the public diplay of personal information, we tried to negotiate before the weighing. Surely, it was a HIPPA violation. Another common ploy was for one to offer the latest measurement from their last doctor's appointment. That tactic failed.

Will believed no one. Will believed in safety in numbers. And I believed in Will.

We crossed the tarmac to the single-engine, six-seat plane anchored to hooks in the concrete so it wouldn't blow over. We used the small metal step beneath the fuselage to lift ourselves up to the door large enough to allow, at most, a 300-pound person to squeeze through. After we all made it inside, we settled into our assigned seats. I sat in the copilot seat, Joe and Howard took the middle two, and Sarah sat in the rear with some of the luggage, since she was the lightest.

Once our five-point seat belts were fastened, we taxied to the same runway on which we had just landed. Every bump and irregularity of the runway vibrated through the frame of the plane and into the frames of our bodies. It was like being in a Porsche, where you could feel everything, instead of a stretch limo. I felt the tug and pull of every turn, and the thrill of the thrust that pushed me back into the seat as we accelerated and took off. The sight of tin roofs, dry creek beds, and the charcoal haze of the city below us soon gave way to the aquamarine sea speckled with canoe-like fishing boats, row boats, and single-mast sail boats. Ahead, twenty minutes away, La Gonâve looked like a breaching humpbacked whale. La Gonâve—and all its adventure—awaited me.

CHAPTER 3

Flight to La Gonâve

The twenty-minute flight to La Gonâve gave our tensed muscles and churning minds a chance to relax. From high up in the sky, we were calmed by the hum of the engine and the view of the sea a few thousand feet below us. In the distance, we could see Anse-à-Galet, where we were to land. With an estimated population of 18,000, Anse-à-Galet is a city that extends from the beach into the hillside. Although the clouds threw dark shadows on the isle, when the wind blew them away, we caught sight of a parched terrain. The ground was barren. The tree leaves wore a coat of dust. The drought had turned the entire island brown.

As we approached Anse-à-Galet, we could see crowded tin roofs, a mausoleum, and more smoke from burning charcoal. It was the main cooking fuel. We circled the landing strip, which was a smoothed section of beach parallel to and only about thirty yards inland from the high tide mark. Jonas, the erstwhile air-traffic controller, baggage man, and official greeter stood next to a pole with a windsock, acting as the lone navigational guide. His cinderblock house was nestled between the runway and the water so that he was readily available for his duties. He maintained some semblance of order, but we, nevertheless, buzzed the landing strip to shoo away the playing children, occasional cow, and ever-present dogs. We watched the children scatter into the surrounding brush and wait for the billowing cloud of dust we caused on touchdown to settle before they came out.

We taxied to within thirty feet of a tabby wall and a ten-by-twenty-foot cinderblock building painted green, with a tattered Haitian flag attached at the corner. In front, a hand-painted, white wooden sign stuck in the ground informed us that we were at La Gonâve International Airport. We had arrived. When we exited the plane, Jonas greeted us with a firm handshake, a smile, and a hug. Bowlegged and with only a few remaining teeth, he wore baggy shorts, an orange safety vest over his navy golf shirt, and Nike tennis shoes that had holes where his toes had worn through. "Bonjour," he said.

Next, the children, eager to meet the new visitors to their island, charged out of their hiding places, surrounded us, and shouted, "Blanc, Blanc, Blanc." Subsequently, we heard this chant many times and considered it friendly. Thanks to Sarah, we had bags of Tootsie Roll Pops, Jolly Ranchers, and peppermints to hand out. Everyone got a piece of candy, and some managed to get two. They smiled, laughed and said, "Messi."

During this melee, Jonas managed to haul our bags to the terminal and loaded them into the back of a black pickup truck with rusted side panels, cracked windows, and shiny bald tires. Standing beside it was Claude, who was wearing a pressed white shirt, black slacks, polished black shoes, and a navy blazer. At six-feet-two, Claude, like our new friend at the airport, seemed larger than life. The school administrator and our chauffeur, he spoke excellent English and could be stoned-faced or show you a devilish smile. He became a very good friend.

Saint Francis Episcopal Compound was our destination. The trip to the compound took us through dirt streets, where dogs and children roamed free, pigs wallowed in garbage, and plastic bottles and wrappers danced in the wind. Our adventure became more gut-wrenching as this Third World shock bombarded us. We noticed how so many things that we took for granted back home were missing on La Gonâve. The rutted roads and streets were unpaved. There was no electricity or running water. There is a saying that goes, "Haiti is the land the world forgot and La Gonâve is the land Haiti forgot." Our drive showed us how much truth was in those words.

Our ride ended when Claude honked the horn in front of a solid ten-foot-wide metal gate that slid inside an eight-foot-high concrete wall that surrounded and protected the compound inside. Sequestered within were the church, a school for grades K-12, the rectory, and our guest rooms. This would be our home during our stay. Once inside, we parked and unloaded our bags. From the parking area, we followed Claude along a walkway that seemed like a darkened canyon floor between the two-story walls of the church and a wing of the school.

Climbing up a stairway that allowed only one person to ascend at a time, we reached a narrow second-floor balcony. On the right, directly across the wall of the balcony, were the windows of a few classrooms. They had no glass or screens, but wooden shutters that opened to the inside. Leaning out of them, male students in their uniforms of blue shirts and khaki pants and female students in their uniforms of white blouses and green plaid skirts looked at us. They wanted to practice their English. "Good morning, teacher," they shouted, which is a prominent refrain in their lessons. We returned the greeting, and everyone smiled.

On the left were five bedrooms and two bathrooms. The rooms sat atop the church offices and storage rooms. Two single beds with freshly pressed sheets, a desk, and a wardrobe (if you were lucky) filled each 10 x 12-foot room. Folded towels were neatly placed on top of the pillows. On one wall, a screened window opened to the balcony, and, on the other side, another screened window opened to the street. Both had interior wooden shutters that barely latched. Somehow, I felt very much at home in this simple but brightly lit room.

We then moved to take a look at the bathrooms, which were spartan. Each had a toilet that took four -to five minutes to refill and a sink that was attached to the wall and supported by two wooden posts. Two corner walls and a knee-high blue-tiled wall defined the shower area. The showerhead and a single knob protruded from the wall. The water could be turned on or off. Above, a flowered plastic curtain looped over a metal railing.

We had noticed a two-hundred-gallon, heavy-duty plastic container on the roof above each bathroom. It was part of a complex setup. A diesel-powered generator supplied the electricity for the pump that transported water from a cistern to it, and then it was up to gravity to supply the water pressure. When we ran the water, we discovered that the water temperature was the same as the air temperature. We learned that water conservation mandated the following rules: when showering, the dribbling water can be turned on for an initial wetting and again after one has soaped up for a quick rinsing. The toilets can only be flushed after going number two or after several accumulations of going number one.

The combination of the hot airplane ride, the dusty arrival, the bone-jarring ride on the pickup truck's side rails, and the exposure to abject poverty made me feel like a carpet hanging limp on a line after being beaten on both sides for cleaning. Nothing in the world would have made me feel better than a long, hot shower, but for now, a washrag facial and a short rest before dinner would have to suffice.

Just before the call to dinner, we heard music rising from the area below us. Across the courtyard, Oriel, blind from birth, sat on a folding chair in the doorway of a windowless room, where he lived. His music moved me deeply. He was playing his guitar and singing songs in Creole. A battery-powered keyboard sat next to him, waiting to be played. His pitch was perfect, and the words didn't matter. As the music vibrated my eardrums, it activated the neurons that released feelings of pleasure that seemed to be as cleansing as that missed shower. Like a triangle in the symphony, the dinner bell seemed to enhance Oriel's performance. We descended the stairs and passed by Oriel on our way to the rectory. He sensed our presence, stopped singing, and said, "Bon soirée." It was a kind, genuine, and peaceful greeting.

Dinner continued to improve my mood, beginning with the layout of where we were to eat. The dining room of the rectory had a heavy, rectangular oak table, seating four on each long side and one at each short end. On the table in front of each seat was a white, oval place mat with cutlery on a folded red cotton napkin on the left and a glass turned open side down on the right. Perforated yellow and green plastic domes covered the entrées. Dinner tonight was crispy, deep-fried goat on the bone, sautéed French green beans with sliced onions, fried plantains, watermelon, and a mound of rice. For beverages, we had a choice of bottled water, Coke, or Prestige, a local beer. I began to reassess. What a great Caribbean vacation this might turn out to be! There were a few inconveniences, but crystal blue waters, a well-made room, music on the veranda, and a fine dinner more than compensated. Plus, I planned to do good work.

Our hosts for this visit were Pere Paul and his wife, Ms. St. Jean. Pere Paul was the priest in charge of the ten churches and schools in his parish, while Ms. St. Jean was a nurse and in charge of the medical services and the liaison for the children that needed specialized care in the United States. During dinner, Ms. St. Jean informed us we would take a tour around town tomorrow. Later in the week, we would go into the countryside and visit her clinic up the mountain.

Ms. St. Jean also informed us that our charge for staying here was $45.00 a day. What? Here we were donating our time and expertise (and giving up income at home) to be on this mission trip, and we were expected to pay for room and board. What was this all about? I snapped back to the present moment when I heard Oriel's music suddenly return. Looking for him, I saw that he had moved to the door outside the rectory. I learned our leftovers would be his dinner. Again, I had to reassess. The money that I paid towards dinner would feed Oriel and maybe others too. People like Oriel did things with pride and respect; they were not poor in spirit. Knowing how my money would help, the $45.00 suddenly seemed like a bargain. I had had plenty of food to eat—and plenty of food for thought. It was time to go to bed.

Throughout the night, buzzing mosquitoes, crowing roosters, and banging wooden shutters allowed me only snippets of sleep. When the sun beamed through at 6:00 a.m., I was fully alert and ready to finally shower. A breakfast of sliced boiled eggs on top of spaghetti, bananas, and dry toast awaited me under the plastic domes in the rectory dining room. Peanut butter, citrus jam, and catsup were also available. My favorite part of breakfast was the dark, rich Haitian coffee, which had none of the bitterness that I was used to. After we finished and thanked our cooks, we went to the front of the church and watched the city come alive before we started the tour. It would be a more extensive glimpse of the rest of the town.

CHAPTER 4

The City Tour

Across the dirt street on the edge of the paved city square, there was a cinderblock fountain from which several spigots jumped out all four sides at different heights. It was a modern-day community well. Women surrounded it. Some filled white five-gallon buckets, balanced them on their heads, and took their water back home. Others filled up plastic jugs, roped the handles together, and slung them over their donkeys' backs. They then led them or rode them—sitting sideways on a wooden saddle—back to their homes in the woods. As we observed all this, it seemed as if we had traveled back two thousand years to biblical times. Stories of women at the well, donkeys for transportation, and dusty feet that needed washing came to mind.

Children gathered around the community well. We saw a few young boys reach in with cupped hands to grab a quick drink—or to playfully throw water at one another. At the low-est station stood a nine-year-old girl wearing flip-flops and a tight-fitting maroon dress, which gave her the appearance of being much older. Beside her stood a wheelbarrow with three topless five-gallon buckets lying on their side. The girl patiently waited her turn. Once she filled up her buckets, she skillfully placed them in a tight triangle in the center of the wheelbarrow for good balance. She then wrapped her tiny hands halfway around the thick wooden handles, lifted them slowly, steadied the wobbly wheelbarrow, and pushed it up the rutted road, going somewhere. I wondered where that might be and how often she did this.

Ms. St. Jean arrived, neatly dressed in a khaki pantsuit and a sunflower yellow blouse. These were her traveling clothes. She had errands to run and said that she would like us to ride along in the back of her black pickup truck. She thought it would be the best way to get a sense of the community. I hesitated for a moment. I was still waiting for the Advil I had taken earlier to kick in and lessen the ache of my bruised buttocks and my psyche, which had been bombarded with the abject poverty and harshness of this culture. I thought a Bloody Mary or two might have been a better alternative to the Advil, but it was time to saddle up and ride again.

Ms. St. Jean's first stop was just a few blocks away. We arrived at a cinderblock home with a grey concrete slab of a floor. Ms. St. Jean was there to check on a patient who lived in this one-room home. Standing outside the house were four children, ranging from three to ten years of age. The three boys wore striped T-shirts and no pants. The oldest child, a girl, wore a blank expression. All were barefoot and held hands. Inside, their mother lay curled in the corner on the slab, with only a sheet to buffer its cold, harsh reality. She did not look well. Her facial skin stretched tightly over her high cheekbones. Her dried lips clung to her teeth as she tried to speak. The whites of her eyes were yellow with bilirubin, and her dilated pupils had no light.

Ms. St. Jean quietly approached her and explained that we were doctors. Maybe this was whom we had come to Haiti to help.

She carefully peeled back the edge of her unbuttoned shirt. As she removed her shirt, the breast tumor that had devoured half of her right chest stared at us like a serial killer looking for its next victim. Ms. St. Jean gave her some water and a pill— and then said it was time for us to go. She explained that many people here preferred to die at home. She also told us relatives would care for the children. I thought to myself, *What a difference there is between this place and home.* On La Gonâve, there were no IVs, no monitors, no hospice. In some ways, it seemed as if there was nothing to help people here. We exited. We looked at the children. There was too much to say; there was nothing to say. My gut churned like a cement mixer.

We prepared to get back into the truck. I grabbed the side rail, put one foot on top of the bald tire, and slung my other leg back into the truck. Our next stop was the home of a seamstress who had finished making a special dress for Ms. St. Jean to wear on Easter. We crept through the streets and, thankfully, stopped under a tree, which provided a whisper of shade on a hot, sunny day. This time we stayed in the truck.

As I looked up one of the streets, I was surprised to see the girl in the maroon dress gingerly guiding her precious cargo towards us. Her hands were steady, her arms were relaxed, and her posture was straight. Her legs were propelled by a steady, rhythmic power that kept the water from spilling. Just before she got to us, the wheelbarrow girl took a left turn and pushed her way up a rock-strewn yard to the house next door. Her grandmother sat there, in a white plastic chair next to a white plastic table. As she watched the life-sustaining water arrive, her sun-baked and deeply wrinkled skin framed a toothless, ever-so-slight smile. When the girl had left the well, I had wondered where she was going—and whether or not she would get there with full buckets. Seeing her with her grandmother, I had gotten my answers and had managed a small smile of admiration of my own.

Since we had been stationary for ten or fifteen minutes, we had become the center of curiosity. Shouts of "Blanc, Blanc, Blanc" notified many in the area of our location, and we were soon surrounded by children again, as we had been at the beach landing strip. Once again, we pulled out bags of candy and gave pieces to everyone. We felt like Mardi Gras royalty dispensing goodwill and cheer. It warmed our hearts that the children seemed overjoyed and ready to grab a bit of sweetness. We kept thinking to ourselves, *Let's do it again. Let's be heroes. Let's be adulated.* It felt good to be able to help others in this small but meaningful way.

Even the water girl took note of the action. During her twenty-yard sprint to join the others, her face transformed from one of intense concentration to one of expectant joy. As the crowd grew larger and larger, we realized our supply of Tootsie Roll Pops was inadequate to please all the eager faces. The candy lottery began. The prize would be a ball of hardened sugar on a stick. We tossed what we had, one at a time, into the air, not to watch a scramble ensue or to determine who had the best eye-hand coordination. We did it that way because we did not want to choose who got one when we did not have enough for everyone.

The girl in the maroon dress, the wheelbarrow girl, the water girl, the transformed girl had her outstretched arm and hand mingled and waving with all the others. She was not being as patient as she had been at the well. Instead, she was assertive. Whether it was luck or adroitness or predestination, she jumped and reached out her tiny hand, which could barely hold the thick handle of the wheelbarrow, and grabbed the stick of candy. Her smile was instant, wide and flush with white teeth. With deliberate care, she peeled off the wrapping, revealing the cherry-flavored ball. She licked it and admired its glistening red surface. It seemed, in some sense, that she had deserved or earned it.

Now, my smile was full. I remembered myself as a child at Halloween. Sometimes, I would put the wrapper back on my candy and save it for later. Licking it would insure that my brother would not want any part of it. This girl surprised me. Rather than stow away the candy for herself, she instead turned to a smaller boy and placed the stick in his hand. And the sharing began.

Her hands were working hands, athletic hands, and sharing hands, all at once. Her hands did the work of the heart. They were hands that may have provided more healing than those of a skilled surgeon. I began to question myself: "Who is the hero here? Who should be adulated? Who is teaching whom?" More food for thought.

Ms. St. Jean returned with her new dress and entered the cab. The engine coughed and sputtered like an emphysema patient struggling to rise from a chair before walking. The truck engine finally found the right mixture of air and fuel and moved forward. Finally, we were going to the beach.

We navigated through the area that was home to the poorest of the poor. We rode over narrower and narrower streets, with muddy potholes breeding mosquitoes and who knows what else. Itinerants and squatters inhabited the shacks made of stick and cheap mortar walls, with loosely fastened tin roofs for shelter. For boundary fences, they had wired together stripped-down tree branches of various sizes, lengths, and straightness, which were stuck in the ground. This was beach-front property. It would be prime real estate at home. Here it was free.

In the yards, mother hens kept their chicks in safe proximity. Roosters crowed and puffed out their chests, displaying their feathers with patches of red, yellow, and deep forest green mixed with black and white spots. Scrawny grey-and-white cats lay against the fence, staking their territory. This land filled with animals was the children's playground. Once again, we heard the salutation, "Blanc, Blanc, Blanc." We were bright white. We were on display. We were on a tour. We smiled and waved.

Between this shanty town and the beachfront hedges, we could see a flat expanse of land cleared of rocks and shells. The cleared land served as a kite-flying area, a bike-racing venue, and three soccer fields. Small orange cones designated the soccer field boundaries; stone-filled one-liter soda bottles or anything else that would be noticed as markers were used to define the goals. We were about to make our way across the patch of cleared land when I caught sight of another nine- or ten-year-old girl running barefoot out of her fenced yard and toward us. Shouting, waving, and smiling, she caught up and ran alongside us. Coming up next to me, she stretched out her arm and offered me a piece of flatbread.

I considered it as a gesture of friendship and goodwill. I reached out and took it like a baton exchange. I had no idea how it had been made, where it might have been stored, or who had handled it. I also had no candy to give her in exchange. Nevertheless, when I accepted the bread, I watched her smile growing larger and her eyes reflecting the bright sun. I had planned to put the gift down on the truck bed, but her stride lengthened and quickened as she kept pace with us. Soon, other enthusiastic friends joined her. I now had an audience.

What to do? My original plan to slyly discard the bread now seemed ungrateful. I wondered if I could contract hepatitis, cholera, typhoid, or some other dreaded disease if I ate it. Maybe I could palm it like a magician and pretend to make it disappear in my mouth? But it was too firm and large for that. Maybe the children would drift away? But they were too strong and fast for that. Maybe I could put it in my mouth for a few seconds and then remove it without danger or harm? It would be a reverse five-second rule. That seemed like the most reasonable solution.

The children watched me put the bread in my mouth. They burst forth with louder cheering and clapping and still kept pace with our truck. They would not go away. My five seconds was almost up. Their persistence was challenging me, and I did not know what to do. At that moment, another phrase erupted from the back of my mind, like a volcanic eruption: "Take this bread, eat, and do this in remembrance of me." I swallowed it. I felt the hard piece of bread slide down my throat. A rush of adrenaline surged like magma from my gut and coursed through my veins. I felt the adrenaline make the hairs on my arms, neck, and back stand up. A sense of joy, exhilaration, and peace alleviated any concerns about the safety of what I had done.

When the children saw me accept their hospitality, they stopped running—but kept waving and smiling. I waved and shouted back, "Au revoir. Merci beaucoup."

CHAPTER 5

The Beach and the Mountain

Ms. St. Jean wanted to show us where we could swim and relax in the future. We slowly distanced ourselves from the children, traversed the open field, and headed for an opening in a dense row of bushes that separated the field from the beach. It was a narrow strip of sand, shells, coral, and washed-up plastic bottles. She crept along until we stopped at a leafless, crooked tree standing alone at the water's edge. It served as a clothes-drying rack and marked the spot where we would be able to safely wade into the warm, clear, refreshing Caribbean Sea. The ocean floor was thick with plant life that hid sharp coral and spiny sea urchins. A singular entry path had been worn from the shore to deeper water in order to try to preserve the underwater life already threatened by pollution. It was still necessary to have some sort of footwear to avoid cuts and stings. Tennis shoes or docksiders would work, but the best would be an all-purpose sandal, like a Teva or Keene, that would dry quickly. We did not swim that day, but we took full advantage of the opportunity on many future trips. The young Haitian boys and men, who were excellent swimmers, would join us in a game of keep-away with a Nerf football or a water polo ball. I think it was the girls on our trips in their bikinis that were the attraction, not the sporting games.

Our next stop was the Wesleyan Hospital and Clinic where we met Dr. Kate, a family physician in her early thirties, who had been practicing here for several years. Her husband was an agronomist, and one of his main projects was the development of the drought-resistant Moringa tree and all its benefits, from the prevention of soil erosion by its roots to the nutritional value derived from its leaves.

The hospital was ancient. The nursing station near the entrance contained all the patient charts in neat racks. The nurses wore crisp white dresses, clean white shoes, and smart white caps. They were very professional and greeted us with kind smiles. The two hallways extending out from the nursing station were filled with patients on beds or stretchers. At the present time it was overcrowded, and a majority were being treated for typhoid fever. The patients who were lucky were in a room that had four to six beds. Family members stood or sat with each patient and provided food and water. The hospital had one operating room, which had the only window air conditioner; the labor rooms were nothing more than regular rooms with two cots and where patients might labor side by side. We asked about medical staff. Dr. Kate explained that social doctors were present on a rotating basis for a year, under the direction of the ministry of health as repayment for their medical education, some of which was done in Cuba. Dr. Martinez was the only surgeon and had been there for many years. Nurse Francis was the head nurse and administered spinals for his surgeries. I thought this would be a perfect opportunity to offer our services. We could return and perform surgeries, lighten his load, and help out. Dr. Kate firmly explained that the staff was stretched to the limits and that if we wanted to do surgery, we would need to bring our own staff. I thought our offers would be received with enthusiasm. Once again, an unexpected challenge was presented. I was being forced to deal with a different reality and wasn't quite sure how to do it.

The scenario would repeat itself several years later when I attended the Haiti Connection Conference in Port-au-Prince, where NGOs, the ministry of health, and various other organizations met to share their successes and failures as they addressed the multitude of problems that existed throughout the country. I attended one of the breakout sessions led by Hilda, the dynamic, energetic, and charismatic head of the nursing school there. As I learned about her excellent, certified four-year program with a yearly tuition of $3,000 that graduated 100 percent of her students, I could hardly contain my excitement and admiration. After the presentation, I approached her, thanked her, and asked, "Could you send one of your graduates to La Gonâve? We are in desperate need of one."

She looked me straight in the eye. "You send me a student from La Gonâve, and I'll send her back. Then you'll have your nurse." Another frank, pragmatic, and stunning challenge. She was right. This model would provide the basis for our developing or enhancing programs in the future for nurse midwives, agricultural seminars, and animal husbandry for the goat projects.

But back to our tour. We got back into the truck and

headed to the compound. We passed a mausoleum, with goats climbing over the family headstones. There were barbershops and welding shops and small stores selling soaps, candies, batteries, antacids, wine, and lotto tickets. Over a wall, there was a man making sturdy wooden chairs like those we had at the dining table. In spite of all the abject poverty, commerce existed. The children ran free in the streets and smiled and waved.

We had skipped lunch. By now, I was spent and ready to rest before dinner.

We entered the compound gates, climbed the stairs, and found a cooler with bottled water, Cokes, and Prestige on the veranda. I grabbed a Coke, stretched out, and wondered how we would ever approach this project. Soon, the dinner bell rang.

Tonight the cooks had prepared extra crispy fried chicken, fried plantains, fresh lettuce with sliced tomatoes, and—of course—red beans and rice. I was again astounded by the hospitality and the culinary skills of the young cooks. During dinner, Ms. St. Jean said that tomorrow we would go up the mountain into the countryside and see the Bill Rice Clinic.

That night the wind blew, the shutters banged, the roosters crowed, and the dogs seemed to be waging gang warfare. I tried to read, using a flashlight propped over my shoulder and resting on the pillow. It was quite unsteady and just seemed to attract more mosquitoes and moths. I turned it off and put on more Deet.

The night felt short, and church bells from across the street at 6 a.m. heralded the start of the day. There was still no rain. After a dribble shower and a shave, I was looking forward to coffee and exploring the countryside. We were waiting to be summoned for breakfast when the school band started to play in the courtyard. Claude led with his trombone, Charlot played the snare drum, and a trumpet and clarinet were part of the ensemble. All of the children who had been milling about or entering through the gate from the street organized themselves into groups according to their class. Arranged in their straight lines with their clean, pressed uniforms and backpacks, they resembled a platoon ready for action. After a few inspirational remarks from the headmaster, they sang their national anthem a cappella while the flag was raised. The band struck up a stirring march, and each class, starting with the kindergartners and ending with the twelfth graders, marched single file up the main steps and then peeled off to their classrooms. They showed great pride and enthusiasm. It was enough to make me stand a bit straighter with respect for them and to realize how much they valued some of the things we take for granted.

Breakfast consisted of the usual premier coffee, dry toast with peanut butter or guava jelly, small bananas, and a warm, thin, creamy porridge with a hint of cinnamon. After dining, we loaded the bed of the truck, which already held a spare tire in the center, with boxes of medicines for the clinic, duffle bags with clothes for villagers, and a blue cooler containing water bottles and sandwiches for our lunch. It was a tailgate with a Haitian flair. We hopped on board, sat on the side rails, and headed out the gate. This time, we turned to the right and carefully maneuvered our way through the narrow streets filled with men carrying rebar or bags of cement, women walking with brightly wrapped bundles balanced on their heads, donkeys being led by children who were not in school, and the ever-present dogs milling about. The same sorts of shops we saw yesterday had opened their doors, and small tables were set on the edge of the street, with the goods from inside on display. Some shop owners covered their wares with pieces of cloth to keep the dust off. It wasn't too long before we came upon and had to circumvent a pickup truck propped up on cinder blocks that was waiting for a tire to be replaced. Anse-a-Galet is built into the hillside; as we were creeping up a steep couple of blocks, we stopped. From a side street, the clinic pharmacist and lab technician approached and hopped on board. We had to squish tighter together to make room for them. I still had space to cling to the railing. I wondered if we had more surprise riders ahead. It reminded me of riding the streetcars in San Francisco: riders hopping on and off at random. It took about ten minutes, and we were out of the town and on the open road. On the shoulder, we saw men who mixed sand, gravel, cement, and water on flat wooden panels and who then scooped the mixture into molds, where it would dry. This was their cinder block factory. The few houses that were being built had spectacular views of the sea and mainland Haiti across the bay. Most had one floor done, or partially done, and rebar sticking up in anticipation of an addition.

The road to the clinic was about three miles long, but it took forty-five minutes to get there because of the switchbacks, ruts, narrow curves, and steep inclines. Even at a snail's pace, the jarring caused by the bumps and the crevices resulted in a banging of one's bottom against the hard metal railing. The soreness was worse than the time when we exchanged paddles during fraternity hell week. We'd had the social shock, some sleep deprivation, and now physical abuse. This resembled a boot camp. I began to wonder if it was such a good idea to have come on this trip. I noticed our Haitian companions did not seem to mind any of it. They were talking, laughing, animated in their gestures, and shouting out to friends walking on the road or working in the fields. It seemed as if everyone knew everyone. We came upon another pickup, which was loaded with bags of cement, rebar, and at least ten riders, some of whom had one leg inside the truck and one hanging out of it. They all seemed to be relaxed and enjoying the ride. Obviously, the Haitians had been traveling this way for years, and I noticed none of them held onto the truck as I did. I decided to try to copy their technique. I let go of my death grip to see if I could go with the flow as they seemed to do. I released my hands, stretched my sore fingers, and placed them on my thighs. It worked! My hips synced with the sway and undulation of the truck, and our squished bodies provided cushioning on either side. It was more comfortable and less straining. Maybe I should always consider letting go of other things, not try to control everything, accept the help of others, go with the wind or the current of the sea like ancient mariners, and then adjust as needed. It was another gift from these wonderful yet often ignored people. We followed them until there was a wider spot for them to pull aside just enough to let us pass. Our driver gave them an appreciative honk. I gave them an appreciative wave. It was a relief to get away from their dust.

Upward and onward we went. The higher we went, the more beautiful the views were, and the more impoverished the homes were. Goats darted across the road and into the thicket; off to the side, smoldering mounds of wood and grass produced lump charcoal, which would be gathered into large, grey bags, placed on the road, and later picked up for transport to the mainland. Men used their machetes to till the soil or hack down trees while women scrubbed clothes over washboards and placed the dresses and shirts on thorny bushes to dry; chickens and half-dressed children scampered in the dusty yards. They ran towards us and shouted, "Blanc, Blanc," always with a wave and a smile. We returned the gestures and replied, "Bonjour."

After the trek up the limestone road, we reached a plateau and a fairly smooth dirt road, and our driver goosed the engine for a brief spurt. It was a nice change of pace, kind of like a mini drag race. It was also cooler, and there was more vegetation, since the erosion was less severe. Plots of sorghum, banana trees, and beans struggled to survive the drought, but they hung on for the time being. One last hill to ascend, and we were at the clinic. Another large, heavy metal gate slid open behind a protective cinderblock wall, and we drove in, parked, and eased our way to the ground.

CHAPTER 6

The Bill Rice Clinic

The clinic opened in 2000, eleven years after Bill Rice, a minister from First Presbyterian Church in Atlanta, and Pere Paul, representing the Episcopal Church of Haiti, conceived of the project. They, along with others, combined their efforts to purchase the land and build it near Holy Cross Church at Nouvelle Cite. Their vision was to provide a community health center in the mountains for the rural population.

Inside, there was a waiting room with benches against the front wall, the sidewalls, and down the hallways on either side. On the left was a small nurse's station for triage and check-in. Down the left hall way was a small laboratory, which had a centrifuge, a microscope, and a bottle of chemical strips for urinalysis. Next was the pharmacy, with very few medicines. The exam rooms each had a desk, a chair, and an exam table. In the back, several rooms were empty or filled with donated wheelchairs, crutches, IV poles, hazardous waste receptacles, and lots of surgical supplies that could not be used. How or why it all got here was a mystery. There were a few cots that served as outpatient beds, where dehydrated patients could be given IV fluids.

We unloaded the truck, took the cooler inside, ate our cheese sandwiches, and discussed the situation. Ms. St. Jean informed us that many patients walked to the clinic, either from Anse-a-Galet or from the surrounding villages. Some got up before dawn and hiked for four or five hours to be seen. Once a month, the staff from the clinic would load up the truck with medicines and travel to even more remote areas to provide a mobile clinic. We concluded it would be a daunting task to bring all the appropriate medicines, paper drapes, exam gloves, soaps, speculums, gauze pads, cleaning solutions, and everything else we needed and took for granted at home.

After lunch, she showed us the garden on the hillside and the goat project. Farmers could bring a female goat here, have her meet Joshua, and hopefully go home with the female goat pregnant. When she delivered, the farmer would return one of the female offspring to the project for someone else. All in all, it was a great program, as long as the goats remained healthy. Next, we trekked up the hill to visit the church and school. We passed a woman who squatted beside a charcoal fire on the ground, where she fried plantains, dumplings, and small bits of chicken that the staff purchased for lunch. The lay leaders, teachers, and children greeted us with enthusiastic warmth and thanked us for coming. Again, it was hard to absorb the depth of their gratitude. It was time to head back down the mountain. The staff at the clinic thanked us for coming and hoped we would return soon to see patients and provide them with continuing education. The trip going back was still slow, but much less jarring, and the cooler temperature, combined with the gorgeous views of the sea and valleys, made it almost enjoyable. It was more like riding a Tennessee walking horse than a bucking bronco. Once we were back home, it was a familiar routine: clean up, rest, have a fine dinner, and get ready for tomorrow. Tomorrow was Good Friday—maybe— an appropriate end to our visit.

CHAPTER 7

The Moth

That night, after the bone-jarring rides, my muscles ached and craved a massage. I lay on my stomach, shirtless and sheetless, trying to find a way into sleep. A giant moth lit on my lower spine. My normal response would have been to reach around and brush it off or slap it and flick its lifeless body out the window. After the ride and some new perspectives, I decided to let it be (Mother Mary might be proud of me) and see what happened. With slow, delicate, dainty movements that resembled a feather, ending to a deep-tissue massage, it came up my spine, turned to go over my right shoulder blade, and headed toward my neck. The closer it got to my face, the more I concentrated on being still and devised a plan to separate us if it didn't fly away. When it rested below my ear, I had had enough sensitivity training. I trapped it with my right hand, felt its fluttering efforts to escape, got up, opened the door, and set it free.

CHAPTER 8

Good Friday

The roosters crowed all night, and the morning dawn broke bright. Good Friday services were planned to start at 9 a.m. "Before the rooster crows, you will deny me three times." It was my first thought of the day. We showered, shaved, and enjoyed a cup of coffee on our so-called veranda before breakfast. It was supposed to be a day of rest. Breakfast was leisurely. We were served fried eggs garnished with sliced sweet onions and green peppers, fresh mango, toast, and more coffee. The coffee was becoming addictive. I took another cup back to my room.

Saint Francis Episcopal church was filled to capacity. The men wore suits or sport coats, ties, crisply pressed slacks, and shined shoes. The women were equally well groomed in their brightly colored dresses, hats, and pumps. The children were clean and orderly. I had dressed up as best I could with black pants and a white, semi-pressed, long-sleeved cargo shirt, but I was severely underdressed. I sat on the end of a pew next to Howard.

"I'm feeling conspicuous due to my attire and hope it's not disrespectful."

He leaned toward me and whispered, "Me too. Plus I'm Jewish."

The service began as the priest and the acolytes, in the midst of incense and song, proceeded up to the altar. The people in the congregation seemed to have an innate, natural singing ability, and their voices filled the sanctuary with robust harmonies. The service lasted two hours and was replete with scripture readings, sermons, baptisms, communion, and the collection. Since everything was in French or Creole, the best I could do was to try to absorb the experience by osmosis. During the announcements, Pere Paul took the opportunity to draw us out of hiding and explain our reason for visiting. We were welcomed with smiles, applause, and congregational thank-yous. Later, some of the children left their parents and sat beside us or on our laps and held our hands. They truly did pass the peace.

At 11:30, the final blessing was given, and the final song was sung. We were ready to leave the sanctuary, maybe walk around town, and then start to pack for tomorrow's departure. Outside the front doors, a gentleman in a black suit, black shoes, black shirt, and a red tie approached us, carrying an open Bible and speaking into a battery-enhanced bullhorn. He was apparently the local evangelist calling for all the lost to repent. Simultaneously, across the city square opposite the well, a Catholic priest clad in a white robe and shouldering a wooden beam led his parishioners in a reenactment of the Stations of the Cross on their way to Mass at noon. In a one-block area, we had been exposed to a course of religious diversity tempered with patience and respect. Howard said he was ready for lunch. I agreed.

That night, after dinner and packing, we sat outside the rooms and began to discuss possible future trips and what it would take to actually provide clinical care. It was pitch black, and planets, constellations, and the Milky Way were brilliant and easily identified. From somewhere in the distance, we began to hear the rhythmic beat of what sounded like bongo drums or tom-toms. We wondered what that was all about and listened intently. It got louder and closer. Gradually, other instruments that had a reedlike sound, tambourines, ratchets, and a trumpet joined in. We stood up and tried to look out over the schoolyard, but we could not see anything. With a combination of curiosity and trepidation, we went down the stairs and into the schoolyard. The band, or whatever it was, had stopped outside the wall of our compound. Hand clapping, foot stomping, and singing raised the level of participation, and a new synergy was reached. I had never heard anything like it. Maybe a band in New Orleans or Native American dances would be similar, but this was at a different level. Pere Paul and Ms. St. Jean always locked the gates after dark for our safety, but I wanted to see what was going on, not just hear it. In the corner of the schoolyard, there was a tree right next to the wall. I walked to it, gingerly climbed its fragile branches, grabbed the top of the wall, pulled myself up, and leaned over. The gathering of people, some of whom had been in church this morning, was assembled in front of the house adjacent to the compound. Some held the band instruments that we had not been able to identify. They included bamboo tubes of various lengths that were blown into, gourds filled with seeds that were shaken, and some sort of metal scraper that provided a sharp counterbalance. In the front, a couple resplendent in bright green, yellow, red, and blue flowing robes, in sharp contrast to the white, flowing robes of the

Episcopal and Catholic priests, danced and seemed to be leading the music as well. The front door to the house opened, and a woman came out and gave them some money. The celebration continued for a few minutes and then moved on. What was this? Trick or treat, or caroling, like at Christmas time? No. It was Rara. I would later learn it's an ancient celebration that begins at the end of Carnival or the eve of Lent and that peaks at Easter Week. It's the time of year when the poor can congregate and voice political concerns or other grievances, generally without fear of retribution, but they also conduct a spiritual service that commemorates the descent of angels and saints with Jesus into the underworld on Good Friday.

One more religious layer manifested itself in this singular block. It was time to go to bed.

CHAPTER 9

Leaving La Gonâve

Our few days in La Gonâve were over. It was time to go. We heard the sounds of the plane's engine drift down from the cloudless, royal blue sky as the plane circled above us in the air. We had one more ride in the truck and received one more set of hand waves and salutations of "Blanc, Blanc, Blanc," as we made our way to the airstrip. As the plane landed, I began to try to digest all of the experiences I had just had.

Like food in the stomach that is broken down by the acid and enzymes in the process of digestion, my protective shell was breaking down. My emotional armor, so well-crafted and admired throughout the years, was being challenged by this culture. I thought to myself, *If I don't escape this onslaught, I fear that pain will take over that center of vulnerability buried so deep inside of me, protecting it from hurt for many years.* Holy shit. It was frightening, and I could not explain why I felt that way. I was tired, and I was worn thin. I felt myself being stripped bare, exposing my vulnerable center. I was more than ready to have Will land and take us away.

Jonas and the children arrived to see us off. Will arrived in his usual cloud of dust and taxied toward us. The children surrounded us, probably hoping for candy—but we had no more to give them. One of the young boys looked up at me. His round ebony eyes searched my face. His red hair revealed his iron deficiency. As I watched Jonas carry our much lighter bags to the plane, I felt a soft hand slip into my palm. He gave a slight tug on my hand, as one would do while jigging for Walleyes on a calm northern Minnesota lake. I yearned for some of that coolness in that moment. When he tugged a little harder on my hand, it caused me to turn toward those dusty bushes just a few yards away, where the children hid.

A woman wearing a loose-fitting, tattered, forest-green dress appeared from behind the hedge. Her walk was steady, her posture upright, like a runway model. Her bare feet easily traversed the rocks and sand. Her face was stoic, and her gaze fixed on me like a laser beam as she approached. In her arms, she cradled an infant child no more than one or two months old. She had dressed this baby in a perfectly pressed gown white as fresh snow. The infant's face was clean, free of drool or a runny nose. She continued to capture my eye. She kept approaching until she stopped a foot away from me. Now that she was closer to me, two young girls came and wrapped their arms around her knees. The boy let go of my hand and joined them. They were a family.

The woman bowed slightly to me. Her dress fell away from her body, revealing breasts that were flat, wrinkled, and without milk. The woman turned her palms upward and extended her arms to me. She was letting go; she was trying to give me her baby. In a different time, a baby was left in a basket and later picked from the bull rushes. In this moment, it seemed as if the story hadn't changed. This mother wanted a better life for her child. Maybe she had heard that story or one that was similar. She saw me and had hoped that I could help. While my heart told me to take the baby, I knew that I could not. Instead, I placed my left hand on her shoulder and my right hand on the infant's head so that I could hug them. It was the least I could do. It was the best I could do.

I really needed to get away and process everything that I had just experienced during my few days in La Gonâve. I needed to go home and regroup. And then, after that, I needed to do something else. Maybe I would need to come back.

Jonas guided us through the swarm of half-dressed and bare-footed children clinging to the plane. Since most of our bags were empty from leaving supplies behind, we did not have to go through the dreaded weigh-in process before boarding. We climbed into the cabin, buckled our five-point seat belts, and looked out the windows, where we saw the smiling children and the mother with child retreating to the bushes. I waved, and I suppressed the geyser of tears that felt ready to explode like a ruptured water main. *There's no crying in medicine.*

Will pushed the ignition button. The propeller roared on, and dust kicked up from the parched tarmac, covering the children as they waved and scattered to the hedges. Will then taxied to the end of the runway, turned into the wind, opened the throttle, barreled down the center, and took off. Besides the goods we had brought, what else had we left behind? Innocence, skepticism, empathy, suspicion, and perhaps some goodwill? Would we come back? What good could we do with just one trip? What good would we do if we were to return again? Was our being there for such a brief stay just like the dust we had generated, a mere speck lost in the pervasive combination of wants and needs? These are the questions I asked myself as we pulled further and further away from La Gonâve.

I suspect the Haitians had the same questions for us.

We climbed to a few thousand feet and headed directly to Port-au-Prince. As I sat in the copilot seat with headphones, I listened to Will converse with air traffic control. Landing at Toussaint International was not always as orderly as taking off. Sometimes, larger and faster aircraft would race to the front of the line like a pig shoving its way to the feeding trough or a surgeon declaring his case was more critical and should be bumped ahead. Apparently, first come, first served was the rule of the game. Will was aware of the possible challenges and was ready to acquiesce.

While we were sitting in the cockpit, I learned that Will and his family had lived there for several years and that his children attended school in the city. In general, they felt safe in Port-au-Prince, but they also did not take that safety for granted. On our final approach, we flew over Cité Soleil, the poorest slum, which had been neglected by many and was home to drug deals, gang violence, and poor sanitation. While it was not too dissimilar from those in America, it also somehow seemed worse than the poorest of our cities. Since Cité Soleil is located near the airport, we were low enough to appreciate how crowded it was. With homes whose concrete walls and metal roofs were on top of one anther other—or, if lucky, separated by thin alleys—there was hardly any room to move. The narrow roads did not seem to offer an easy way out.

I wondered what it would be like to live there. Was it possible to escape? Or did one inevitably succumb to the pressures of oppressive heat and lack of adequate food and water—and act in the interest of personal survival, whether those actions were moral or not? If I were in the same situation, would I join a gang, trade knife wounds, or deal in drugs? What would I do to survive? Like a quick slap on the face, my introspection was interrupted by the bounce of the wheels on the runway.

Soon, we were on the ground again. After coming to a stop, we unloaded our gear, exited the ancillary terminal, and caught our van to the main terminal. Check-in and processing were uneventful. At the duty-free shop, we purchased English-Creole dictionaries, Haitian coffee, vanilla, and Rhum Barbancourt. During the flight home, we received the same package of cheese, crackers, raisins, and Toblerone chocolate. On the trip over, it seemed like a perfunctory treat. Now, it seemed like a luxurious and almost decadent indulgence. What other perceptions would change?

Approaching Miami filled me with anticipation, apprehension, and a sense of adventure. Returning to a world of manicured golf courses, personal swimming pools, and clean, wide streets with orderly traffic seemed decadent. Yet all this opulence had a similarity to Port-au-Prince. It was home to its own drug deals, gangs, violent crimes, and slums ignored by many. It was difficult for me to reconcile the vast disparities—yet also similarities—between the coastal cities only a few hundred miles apart.

It was even more difficult to explain any of my changed perceptions to anyone. During a Sunday service after I got back home, I was asked to tell my congregation about my experiences in La Gonâve. This seemed like an impossible feat. I hadn't yet had time to process everything. The images, sights and sounds, and feelings from the trip clamored around in my brain, rendering me unable to articulate anything coherently. I choked. The best I could say was that I hoped others could go on a future trip with me. The road trip had to be experienced to be understood.

In the years to come, many did join me. These are some of those adventures.

CHAPTER 10

Fly Boat

There were three ways we could travel from mainland Haiti to La Gonâve. The quickest, as previously described, was a twenty-minute flight in the six-passenger, single-engine plane. The other two ways were by boat. To make the one-hour-long ride up the coast from the airport to the dock, we needed a taxi van and pickup truck to transport us and our gear. Depending on the time of day, we would either go directly there, load the boat, and speed across the bay, or spend the night in a resort nearby before leaving the next morning.

Traveling by a sailboat ferry, the least desirable option, would take three hours, and the ferry would be overcrowded with men and women. Bringing their goats, roosters, large bags of rice, pallets of bottled water and Coke, fresh bunches of green bananas attached to their branches, and other fresh fruits and vegetables, they carried all the goods that they intended to sell at roadside stands on board with them. For them, every day was a farmer's market. They kept the most precious goods in their laps to avoid loss or damage, guarding them against others' gazes.

The second option was to take a fly boat. Taking the fly boat allowed us to transport with us all our duffle bags filled with new shoes and Crocs for the children, medical supplies for the clinic, musical instruments for the school band, clothes for all ages, and six treadle sewing machines for a new co-op. And it was fun. The hour-long crossing, where we skimmed across the waves as the wind whistled through our hair and the saltwater sprayed on our faces rivaled a chartered Caribbean cruise.

We had chosen a fly boat named the *Papillon*. The butterfly painted on the side was scraped from the many trips it had taken across the waves, and its wings were shredded like a poorly displayed entomology specimen. The bow had a flat area that provided a protective covering for dry storage and that served as the landing spot for boarding and unloading. Two outboard engines were mounted to the stern. Each motor was supplied fuel by a clear plastic tube that snaked out of a rag that was stuffed into the top of a red freestanding gasoline can. It was a makeshift setup.

A crew member wearing flip-flops, loose-fitting knee-length red shorts, and an unbuttoned white short-sleeved shirt served as our navigator. He straddled the apex of the bow, looked for sandbars and unexpected large waves, and pointed right or left when he wanted the captain to alter the course. He was assisted by a first mate, who was barefoot and wore cutoff khakis and a tight-fitting black T-shirt that proclaimed, "Elvis Lives." If one of the motors sputtered, the first mate would calmly switch the tubing to a fresh gasoline supply.

Our duffel bags were stacked in a wide well between the covered cargo area and the captain's command post. Our backpacks, meanwhile, were tossed into dry storage and covered with a blue plastic tarp. The Episcopal priest on board, who was in charge of several churches and schools on La Gonâve, was our boss man. Though he did not wear his clerical collar, he still wore black long trousers and a polo shirt. The priest made sure that all of our bags were loaded by the strong, agile teenage boys who tossed them as if they were down pillows and paid their boss man.

Our group was comprised of medical personnel, teachers, the church's minister and minister of music, and young and old adventurers. For some, it was their first trip. For others, it was their second, third, fourth… or more. When boarding, we gingerly stepped from the dock and onto the bobbing bow, accepted the stabilizing hand of the captain. The captain directed us to sit as far back and as close to each other as possible, so as to counterbalance the excess weight up front. With a slight smile and a lighthearted inflection, I asked if everyone could swim. Clifford, a sixty-six-year-old fellow Scandinavian, with a full head of wavy grey hair, piercing blue eyes, and a dry sense of humor, winked and answered, "No."

Once seated on a wooden bench on either side of the ship, running from bow to stern, we took in the wonder of the ocean and the sky around us. The calm aquamarine sea and the bright blue sky mirrored each other, like identical twins. The sea breeze was as soft as that from a ceiling fan on a wraparound porch. Looking at the orange and yellow life vests piled in the center hold with our bags, we got an idea for seating. Although all of the life vests were smudged with oil stains, they made excellent cushions for our backs or bottoms.

We shoved off from the dock. We felt that the boat was sitting lower on the water than usual. The captain motioned with his arms that we needed to move further back to counterbalance the front-end load. We turned sideways, slid back, and crammed ourselves even closer as we obeyed his command. Once he was satisfied with the distribution, he throttled the engines from idle to acceleration. As we gained speed, the bow slowly started to rise.

Fifteen minutes into the crossing, we came upon the sailboat ferry that had left an hour before. We were at full speed and waved with enthusiasm as we came along its side and started to overtake it. Even our captain and first mate seemed excited, joyously shouting in Creole as we passed by. At first, I thought they were taunting the sailors on the sailboat ferry and were boasting about the superiority of their fly boat. But then I noticed the first mate holding a one-gallon plastic milk carton by the handle. The top had been cut off at an angle. While it was not unusual for him to scoop out the excess water that splashed over the side and refreshed us, he was bailing with more intensity and vigor than usual.

Like a coxswain in a crew boat, I thought that he was shouting instructions to the captain to increase the speed. Suddenly, our boss man, the priest, asked me to move up by him. The captain had informed him that there was a small hole in the back of the boat. We were taking on more water than the first mate could keep up with, and we could not go any faster. We were going to circle the ferry, adjust our speed to the ferry's, come alongside it, and then stop and transfer ourselves to it. Since a sea rescue was not on our agenda, none of us wore the life jackets that we had been using for cushions.

As we approached the ferry, the passengers on board looked none too pleased to slow down. I could imagine them thinking to themselves, *You have already overloaded one boat—and now you are going to overload ours.* I relayed the plan and asked Clifford if he was kidding or if he really could not swim. Without a wink or crooked smile, he looked down and said he could not. The priest cupped his hand in front of my ear and whispered, "I can't, either." They were not kidding.

We quickly came up with a plan for transferring ourselves to the ferry boat. The priest would go first, followed by Clifford, the rest of us, and, finally, the bags. Clifford stepped between, around, and over legs, laps, and bags on his way to the bow. He reached up to grasp the strong black arms extended across the side of the ferry. As the strong arms lifted him up and over, his white hair, shirt, shorts, and legs resembled a giant flag of surrender. They placed him below the side rail, next to a woman holding a white cloth in her lap. All subsequent boarders and bags passed over or through them. Once in a while, they served as stepping-stones. Every time Clifford looked up to see what was happening, he had to duck down to avoid being hit.

In spite of being overcrowded like an elevator jammed full of people, the ferry passengers found spaces that didn't seem to exist before, accommodating all the bags and all of us. The sewing machines were the most difficult to transport because of their weight and awkward shape. In the end, there were no injuries, and no cargo was lost. After everyone and everything had been transferred, the fly boat sat high and could gather enough speed to hydroplane home for proper repairs.

We set sail, and all seemed good, but it was only a few minutes until the exhilaration of skimming across the bay was replaced by a slow, steady, and rocky journey. Beads of sweat replaced the cool splash of dispersed waves on our faces. Feeling the heat and sway of the vessel, we felt the specter of seasickness. Our hosts and hostesses seemed to sense our dismay and began to sing and adjust their positions when-ever we needed to stretch or move. They could not have been more hospitable. All in all, we were able to maintain proper decorum.

Their hospitality gave me pause. Would I have done the same? Or would I have thought that the boat could take no more and refused to help? Would I tell the fly boat captain to turn back to shore. The entire scene, with bodies sitting on one another, draped over one another, with arms and legs hanging over the edges of ferry, reminded me of newsreel clips of the Haitian boat people landing on our shores. We were faced with only two hours of this kind of intimacy. It was hard to imagine what stresses those who did it for days endured only to be turned away.

I looked down at Clifford, who had been bent over and wedged between the side of the boat and the woman, and I asked if he needed to move. He said he was okay, but he nodded toward the woman next to him. The white cloth she cradled in her lap had turned blood red, like a lap pad that had mopped up an intraabdominal hemorrhage. I wondered if she had been injured during our rescue.

The woman opened the corners of the cloth, looked up, and showed me two dozen crushed tomatoes. She cried. Her most precious cargo had been destroyed. When we got to shore, we arranged with the priest to buy her entire stock. Fresh salsa was in our future.

CHAPTER 11

Tap-Tap

On one of our trips back home, we had to use the predawn ferry from La Gonâve to the mainland. The flights for that day were booked, and the choppy waters in the channel were not safe for the fly boat.

We had used the predawn ferry before. This was a typical large, diesel-powered ferry that we were used to seeing in the news or in places like Nantucket. We could either sit below the deck or above it. Below deck, the seats were wooden benches, with space underneath for the storage of backpacks, charcoal, and chickens in burlap bags. On the lower deck, the goats were sequestered in the rear, with their legs tied. Most of the people and animals down there were quiet, wanting to rest. Those who were awake could watch a French crime movie playing on a TV above the front door.

Each trip seemed to have its own share of events and stresses. We always preferred sitting on the open top deck. It was cooler, and watching the early rays of sun slide over the top of the mountains was a peaceful experience. The calm, steady ride provided a time for reflection on how the week had gone. We reminisced about the patients we'd seen, the children's joy and enthusiasm in school and at play, and the progress that had been accomplished with various civic projects. Still, we looked forward to the lounge at the airport, where ham-and-cheese paninis, lattes, Haitian coffee and vanilla, mementos, and duty-free shopping were available.

The wind was more robust than usual. The usually calm bay where we were anchored undulated with the remnants of larger waves from the channel, breaking up only when they spent themselves in the mangroves. The narrow wooden plank from the dock to the ferry bobbed and challenged our balancing skills. Agile boatmen grabbed our large bags and put them below. We started to climb the steps to the upper deck. The captain said we had to go below, as well. After some negotiation with our translator, he reassured us that we could come up later.

We joined the Haitians and all their goods below deck. Once again, we were jammed together, and now the aisles were so filled with baggage that no passengers could leave their seats. Above the benches against the walls were sliding windows that could provide only a snippet of fresh air, which was insufficient for combating the mixture of noxious diesel fumes and sweaty body and animal odors. It made me wonder how Noah sailed for forty days, staying locked inside his boat as rain flooded the earth.

We donned the uncomfortable life jackets before the boat cast off and chugged into open waters. The boat heaved fore and aft and swayed side to side as it fought the raucous waves, like a real-life version of Disney's *Pirates of the Caribbean*. Suddenly, water began to spray and then splashed through the open windows. Those who were getting drenched reached up and shut the windows. The captain closed the front entry door for the same reason. Water was cascading down the steps and onto the floor.

The temperature and the intensity of the odors increased. The dis-ease of many became evident. Some began to sing, while others prayed or simply hung their heads between their knees to try to stave off seasickness. Those who succumbed were considerate enough to hold a towel, a bandana, or a hat over their mouths. Some held tight to the arm or leg of a loved one or their neighbor. Each of us did what we thought would make us feel better in a moment of extreme discomfort.

Looking out the window, I caught sight of small, porpoise-like fish flying by the window. In this moment of despair, I wasn't sure if they were racing one another, escorting one another, or warning us. We were all aware of ferries having sunk. The thought that the ship might sink couldn't help but cross our minds in this moment.

It was a time for analysis. The windows were too small to squeeze through. The door, meanwhile, would be held in place by the force of the water. And even if we managed to get it open, it would buy only a small amount of time, until we all were trapped between the ceiling and the rising water, gasping for that last sliver of air. Eventually, like candles put out by an acolyte, each breath would be extinguished.

Anxiety was useless. It was a time for reflection. If this was going to be the end, then what loose ends were there left for me to tie? Any monetary considerations would be taken care of by accountants, lawyers, and the banks. Any unfinished projects would be completed by others or abandoned entirely. What about frayed relationships that no one could fix from afar? Those loose ends would be left dangling, like half-shredded pieces of paper. Maybe, if we got through this, it would be a good idea for me to trim those loose ends once I returned home. For an hour and forty-five minutes, I pondered these quandaries.

I looked out the window again. The flying fish had disappeared. The pitching and yawing of the boat transitioned to a gentle sway. The roar of the engines diminished. The side of the ferry thumped against the dock. The captain opened the door. We had been delivered. Everyone exited in a pensive and orderly fashion. We had been given another chance at living. Maybe this was like Jonah and the whale. The fare for each of us was one dollar, but we also got the experiences of Noah and Jonah with one trip. These lessons were priceless.

For those two hours on the ferryboat, reality had been suspended. Now it returned with brute force. We looked around for Charles, our driver, who would take us to the airport, but he was not there. It was 8 a.m. Our flight was at 12:30, meaning we had only two hours to get to the airport for check-in. We grabbed our bags and carried them from the dock up the ramp to the road.

This short walk always entailed the challenge of avoiding or rejecting the local entrepreneurs' efforts to sell us small paintings of the Haitian countryside, varnished conch shells, or bracelets with HAITI embroidered in the center. The entrepreneurs offered them in any color combination and could customize one on the spot in the colors of your choice. Most of us had made use of this service in the past and had no need for it this time. One of the more persistent artists accompanied us and kept trying. He spoke fairly good English, so I knew he knew we were not interested. If Charles was there, he would have been able to convince him.

Where was Charles? He had never been late. Suddenly

my Nokia cell phone, which had a SIM card programmed for Haiti, rang. It was Charles. There was a manifestation in Cabaret, a town midway between the airport and us. We would call it a demonstration. The locals were protesting what they considered to be an unfair distribution of electrical services. By blocking the road, they prevented the more affluent residents of Port-Au-Prince from reaching the beach resorts for the weekend. The single highway was completely blocked by abandoned dump trucks, which had mysteriously suffered flat tires in the middle of the night. The drivers, meanwhile, were nowhere to be found. The road was a no-go.

If we could hire a tap-tap to take us to Cabaret, we could walk around the trucks and make our connection. The tap taps available were small pickup trucks, each with a covered bed, which had benches along each side and against the cab. They were brightly painted and displayed religious figures or verses. They served as communal taxis and were not endorsed by the US State Department as a means of safe travel. *Well, I thought to myself, We just survived a dramatic ferry ride. Why not try our luck one more time and catch a tap-tap to Cabaret?*

I looked for our artist, since I needed him to translate. He had gone back to the dock. I spotted him having an intense conversation with a young girl, who was wearing white plastic mesh shoes, black shorts, a white halter top with red polka dots, and Ray Ban sunglasses. She looked like a Haitian Daisy Duke.

I hesitated to interrupt, but I finally called out, "Mon ami."

He reached into his pocket and pulled out the bracelets. I said, "No, merci," and explained, with gestures and mixed English and Creole, that we wanted to hire a tap-tap.

He nodded that he understood.

The five of us followed the artist to the road. He approached one of the taxis, which was already completely full. He knocked on the window and spoke to the driver. He returned and said the driver would take us for thirty American dollars. I agreed. He shouted back to the driver, who got out of the cab and cleared out the current occupants. While this seemed a bit unfair, we had no other choice, since there was not room enough for all of us. We could not waste any more time if we hoped to catch our flight.

I gave mon ami six five-dollar bills. He approached the driver, who had gotten back into the cab. With hands as quick as those of a magician or a backstreet fighter with a switch-blade, he gave him one of the fives and deftly pocketed the others. At first, I was stunned and felt the driver and I had been scammed. I told him, "I saw that." He just smiled and shrugged his shoulders. Then I thought, *He is a shrewd businessman. He negotiated with both the driver and me. We all got what we had wanted.* My lack of language skills cost me twenty-five dollars. C'est la vie.

We secured the large bags to the roof and loaded ourselves into the cramped back end. Then the disembarked passengers joined us in the tap-tap. Two of them stood on the back bumper and held onto the side windows. Once again, I was struck by the lack of personal space in Haiti. Somehow, we all fitted into the tap-tap. The engine came to life, coughing and sputtering like an asthmatic starting to take a morning shower. The driver shifted through the gears and eased onto the highway. *After we get to Cabaret,* I thought, *I'll be ready for a glass of Cabernet.*

We arrived there in about thirty minutes and were confronted with another challenge. The north and south ends of town were both blocked. I had planned to call Charles, but my phone battery was dead. We would have to unload and then walk the mile, dragging our suitcases until we found Charles. The street markets were open and crowded with merchants selling shoes, dresses, belts, soaps, candies, plastic bags of water, fruits, vegetables, and four-foot-long stalks of raw sugar cane. We would have to navigate this maze in order to reach the van.

We went behind one of the disabled trucks and began to weave our way through the boisterous bartering vendors and shoppers. Out of nowhere, a girl of about fifteen arrived at my side. She had a cell phone and motioned for us to follow her. I had no idea how or why she found us. But then it dawned on me that five white Americans dragging suitcases probably weren't too hard to identify. The girl took us through the back neighborhoods and finally to the southern blockade. It was a much more efficient and calm route. She said, "Au revoir," and turned to leave. I reached into my backpack and found the hidden money pouch, which had only twenty-dollar bills left. Folding one in my palm, I shook her hand and said, "Merci."

The chaotic northbound lane of the highway lay ahead of us. Cars and trucks were parked two abreast and backed up for several miles, their drivers and passengers milling about. There was no honking or yelling. Everyone hoped the barriers would be moved soon. Amidst the chaos, Charles spotted us, took us to his van, and helped us load up our gear one more time. He convinced four or five drivers in front and in back of him to inch closer together, which provided just enough room for him to execute a seven-point turn and transfer to the open southbound lane. We settled into our seats.

"Charles, a young girl spotted us in the marketplace and then led us here. Did you call her to help us?"

"No, I don't know anything about it."

"Maybe the priest called her. Maybe the artist called her.

Maybe she just saw us and acted on her own. We're glad she was there."

As we got onto the road, I felt the van's cool air rush out of the vents, washing over me like a cold, rushing mountain stream and making the trip to the airport refreshing.

When we got to the airport, we checked in, went through security, took the escalator to the upstairs lounge, and ordered a ham and cheese sub, a Coke, and fries. It was deli comfort.

CHAPTER 12

To Go or Not to Go

On Tuesday January 12, 2010, an earthquake measuring 7.0 on the Richter scale devastated Haiti.

Several months before, a group of eleven from a large Atlanta Presbyterian Church had planned their annual mission trip for January 8 through January 15. Claire, the designated leader, had been doing this trip for twelve years. This time, they were partnering with Childspring, an organization that had arranged and paid for children on La Gonâve to be treated for clubbed feet, cleft palates, or congenital heart defects. As executive director of Childspring, Rose Emily had travelled to La Gonâve many times herself. She had planned a major celebration to be held on Wednesday the 13th, for those who had been treated and those who would be treated.

Since most in their travel group were first-timers, Claire and Rose Emily asked me to join them. They said that they could use my help and that I could follow up on patients I had seen on previous visits. I had traveled with each of them before and had enjoyed their company. But this would be a different kind of trip than before. As this was a church trip, the group would be much larger than I was used to, which meant there would be more to coordinate. It can be exhausting making sure that all the group members started their antimalarial meds, arrived early enough for departure, packed bags that all weighed fifty pounds or less, had valid passports, and brought a hundred dollars in ones for possible emergencies. Frankly, I was tired of group travel and just wanted to go solo for a change. To go or not to go, that was the question. I said I would go, but my heart was not in it.

The trip was five weeks away. It was Black Friday, and I decided to go to the outlet malls to purchase holiday gifts for my partners and staff. I walked by the basket store and thought, *This is perfect.* I picked out fifteen baskets and filled each of them with various combinations of cold-pressed Italian olive oil, balsamic vinegar from Napa, thimble-sized jars of saffron, lavender-scented hand creams from Provence, and chocolate truffles. The clerks smiled, gave me an additional discount, and then suggested I drive around to the back door for pickup. They had put red bows on the tops of all the plastic-encased gifts and carefully placed them into the cargo area and back seat of my SUV. These would be the perfect gifts. Mission accomplished.

It was 8:45 p.m., and the sun had set long ago. There was no moonlight. It was, after all, Black Friday. Driving home, I felt like a racecar driver, weaving in and out of heavy traffic, chasing down the next vehicle. Oblivious to my speed, I approached a white panel truck and goosed the engine a bit more to pass it on the left.

Unfortunately, the truck blocked me from seeing the fifty-five-miles-per-hour speed limit sign. As I zoomed by, I saw a patrol car parked on the right shoulder. The truck did not block me from the patrol car's laser beam. I saw the flashing blue lights and was chagrined to see I was going eighty-five-miles per hour, a superspeeder violation. I was pulled over by the patrol officer, and I parked on the right shoulder. Unfortunately, Officer Colbert was not impressed with my load of goodwill or my request for a warning. He wrote the ticket.

It was Black Friday.

To go or not to go to court was the next challenge. Speeding and reckless driving were the charges. The court date was set: January 8. That date seemed so familiar in my mind. And then it hit me: January 8 was the scheduled departure date for Haiti. My options were to pay the $375 fine online or to contest his laser readings in court. I had heard that if Officer Colbert didn't show up at court, my case would be dismissed. I had just cleared my record from a series of tickets and did not relish the thought of another three years of increased insurance premiums. I wanted to go to court.

The question of to go or not to go to Haiti hovered over my head. I could easily leave for Haiti a day later, but I did not want it known that "reckless driving" was the reason. Then I got another idea. January 8 also the day a patient of mine was scheduled for a repeat Cesarean section. Previously, I had told her that my partner would do the delivery since I would be going to Haiti. Now I could do the surgery myself—and it would be a perfect cover story for me not leaving with the group.

All of the answers to go or not to go seemed to be falling into place. I could go to the operating room for the C-section, and my patient would be most appreciative to see me again. I could go to court and seek a positive resolution of my charges. I could go on the trip flying solo. Perfect. *The Three A-Me-*

Goes, I thought to myself, remembering my Three Amigos group from my first trip to Haiti.

January 8 started with supportive maternal and paternal grandparents joining the expectant parents in the pre-op room. Their two daughters, aged eight and ten, were making plans to be minimoms. All happily anticipated the birth of the first male in a long lineage of female dominance. In the operating room, the anesthesiologist did her usual excellent job of providing epidural anesthesia, resulting in numbness from the toes to the umbilicus. The abdominal wall was prepped with garnet-colored betadine solution, and sterile, sky-blue paper drapes were positioned to frame the incision site in a rectangle. Everyone in the room identified him or herself and confirmed that we should go ahead with the intended procedure. With a final pinch of the skin, we confirmed that our patient had no pain. We could begin.

The cold and sharp steel blade on the knife handle split the skin of the lower abdomen from left to right. Sliding through slippery, bright yellow globules of subcutaneous adipose tissue, it exposed the glistening white fascia that protects the abdominal muscles. The incision continued until we identified and carefully opened the Saran Wrap-like peritoneal sack that encases all the internal organs. The soft, purplish uterus, once home to us all, was there and ready to be entered. First, I reflected the bladder flap inferiorly so the thinner, lower uterine segment could be accessed. Next, I made a transverse incision of about two inches in the center so that I could insert two index fingers inside and extend it bilaterally. Finally, I used an Allis clamp to create a hole and released the gushing fluid from the bag of water that housed the unsuspecting boy. The heir of the family name was about to arrive. In just a few seconds, he would be born.

I slid my hand into the uterine cavity, using my fingers and palm to cup the back of his head. As I lifted him up, I watched him leave the warm, dark, peaceful, spalike environment. Taking a green rubber suction bulb, I removed the last taste of salty amniotic fluid from his mouth. The bright lights of the operating room and the camera flashes from the family paparazzi greeted his newly open eyes. Strange, new sounds of laughter, cheers, and cries of joy replaced the calm swishing of the placental vessels and the rhythmic cadence of his mother's heartbeats that he had known in the womb. The cold air of the operating room made his wet skin shiver. This was his introduction to life and a new reality.

A few hours later, I returned to tell his mom that I would still be going to Haiti and that my partners would care for her. She thanked me and wished me luck on my trip. The family had gathered around the newborn, who was now wrapped in a snug, warm blanket and wearing a blue stocking cap on his head that resembled a crown. This new little prince was holding court.

I didn't tell them I was headed to court, as well.

At 1 p.m., the judge rapped his gavel. He sat behind an elevated desk, with a computer in front of him. He treated his courtroom like a college classroom, scanning over about 120 freestanding chairs set in a semicircle occupied by felons, near felons, and traffic violators. I was in the back-left area and was relieved to not spot Officer Colbert among the uniformed attendees. I was optimistic about beating the charges. I felt less optimistic about the drug offenders, who were dressed in orange and wore ankle shackles. I watched each of them approaching the bench with a uniformed bailiff and a well-dressed lawyer, pleading not guilty, and getting assigned a court date.

Once all the drug offenders were all processed, the judge offered us traffic violators three responses when our violations were read out loud. Option one was that I could plead guilty and pay the fine. Option two was that I could plead not guilty, and a court date would be set to determine a final verdict. Option three was that I could plead no contest, go to another room, meet with a negotiator, and resolve the issue.

Since I did not want to set another court date, I took option three. The negotiation was one-sided, direct, and simple. The result was that the estimated speed would be reduced to eliminate the reckless driving charge. No points would be assessed on my driver's license, but I would still have to pay the full fine. I took the deal. Two goes were down, and now there was one more go to go: Haiti.

The itinerary was straightforward. On Saturday, I flew to Miami and spent the night in the airport hotel. Sunday, I flew to Port-au-Prince and then hopped over to La Gonâve. It all went smoothly.

When I arrived, Jonas was at the beach. Claude was there to drive me along the familiar rutted streets, teeming with smiling children and lazy dogs. The smell of charcoal always brought back memories of my first trip, just as the aroma of sizzling bacon in the morning brought back memories of breakfast at my grandmother's farm. The warmth of these blended memories blunted the reality of the poverty in Haiti.

We arrived at the compound, where Mass was underway. Since the church service was already half over, I sauntered in through the side door and quietly joined my Haitian and American friends, sitting on the handmade wooden benches that filled the sanctuary. Not missing a beat, Claude took his trombone and resumed his position as music director in the right-front area. I was glad to see Oriel up there, too, wearing his sunglasses and playing the electric keyboard. Charlot, a senior in the high school, played the drums. It was all so comfortable and familiar that it almost seemed like going home.

After the service, we headed to the rectory for lunch. We had fried chicken, pikliz (the Haitian version of coleslaw), fresh mango slices, rice, and beans. We spent the afternoon organizing supplies to take to the clinic and then to various communities during the busy week ahead. On Monday through Thursday, my time would be spent seeing patients in the clinic, with some possible consults or surgery at the hospital in the evenings or early mornings. On Thursday, we planned to return to Port-au-Prince and spend the night at Hotel Montana, where one can have a hot shower, a massage, and an air-conditioned room.

Hotel Montana is a five-star resort where the rich and famous and heads of state come to converse, make deals, and drink and dine. Its multistoried levels are nestled into the hillside high above the city, where the open-air pools and terraces overlook the shanties below. In the hillside, both the privileged and the impoverished share a magnificent view of the brilliant yellow sun turning to amber, as it seems to extinguish itself at the far edge of the sea. Nature avails itself equally to all. A night at the hotel would be the perfect way to decompress before heading home on Friday.

All went according to plan on Monday. After the bone-jarring ride up the mountain to the clinic, I restocked the pharmacy with the medicines I had brought, saw sixty patients, and came back down for dinner. All looked and felt good; everything was going according to plan. I was in a groove. But Tuesday the 12th loomed like a hidden monster anxious to pounce on its unsuspecting victims. Tomorrow, the plan would be disrupted and would require improvisation.

Tuesday morning began with strong coffee, in preparation for another long day. I once again made the bumpy ride to the clinic, saw another forty patients, and rode in the front seat back to the compound in what I thought was just another routine day. I climbed the steps to the so-called veranda, where we were waiting for dinner; I took in the peaceful scene in front of me. Some people were reading, while others were resting. Some were drinking Prestige, while others were drinking rum and Coke. I sat on a metal folding chair, stretched my legs, and rested my feet on another one. We shared stories of what we had done that day. Claire and her crew had built desks for their school. Rose Emily had finalized preparations for tomorrow's celebrations. Everyone had been busy and productive, and we were relaxed.

Our peaceful respite ended at 4:43 p.m. Suddenly, I heard a rumble that sounded like a large truck pounding over a wooden bridge. The building shook like the ground, creating the sensation of lying near a railroad track as a train speeds by. A Coke bottle somersaulted off the ledge and crashed below, like a diver landing a belly flop. "Earthquake!" all of us yelled, and we scrambled to get down the stairs and off the veranda.

We sped down the stairs and rushed to the open courtyard. Claude ran out of his office and joined us. He told us that the local cell phones were not working. Since we, at best, had intermittent cell phone connections back to the States, we started worrying about getting in touch with our loved ones. Some started wondering about getting home at all. Some of us wondered about aftershocks. Rose Emily still anticipated tomorrow's planned Childspring celebration of each child's new life.

After the initial shockwaves had finished, we inspected the buildings. We found cracks in some of the classroom walls and the church bell tower, but we were relieved to discover no major collapses. In town, some of the poorly constructed walls had collapsed. The monster had come out of hiding, but it had not yet revealed its full capacity for horror. It would be another twenty-four hours before we would know that there had been more devastation than could be imagined throughout the island.

That night, we decided not to sleep in the guest rooms, as aftershocks kept coming like the lunges of a chained, rabid dog still trying to inflict harm. Some retired to the unscathed rectory and slept on the floor or shared a bed. Others took a sheet to the open ground and lay flat, feeling the ripples of the earth below from head to toe, like a vibrating bed. No quarters were required. This was a free massage.

In the morning, I went over to the hospital to see if they had any new information. Don, the director of missions, had a satellite phone. He learned that there had been significant damage in Port-au-Prince. While we did not yet know the full extent of the damage, we did learn that the airport was closed on account of the earthquake. I came back and shared the information with everyone. I thought that we, at worst, might have to spend a couple of extra days before getting home. This turned out to be another tremendous misconception on my part.

That afternoon, it was time for the Childspring party. Red, white, and blue crepe paper streamers were draped across a cement wall that separated the schoolyard from a narrow path and crowded homes on the other side. Balloons of all colors were strung from tree limbs in preparation for the celebration and a reunion of sorts. Soon the children and their parents arrived. The young boys wore suits with ties and polished black or brown shoes. The girls came in clean, pressed dresses.

Some were frilly, while others were straight and monochromatic. Almost all of them wore black Mary Jane shoes with white ankle socks. They had worn their Sunday best.

After everyone arrived, we moved onto the awards ceremony. Each recipient was called to the front of the gathering, where Rose Emily recounted his or her malady and subsequent recovery. The child then received a framed certificate of graduation. The church ensemble provided the music for each child as he or she walked forward. There was clapping and cheering for each recipient. This was a celebration of new life. And it was. But across the wall, an equal and opposite force readied itself.

For now, I focused on the ceremony. Domana was the first to be called. Five years ago, her father, a voodoo practitioner, had draped her edematous body over a donkey and brought her to a Childspring representative for help. He told the representative that his traditional herbal remedies had not worked. Domana had heart failure because of a congenital defective aortic valve. She had accumulated thirty pounds of fluid in her legs and abdomen and was unable to walk. She could barely breathe. Fluid filled her lungs and was slowly drowning her. She was subsequently taken to the United States for a successful valve replacement. Now eighteen, she was beautiful and healthy and had a spitfire personality. She wanted to move to the States and be a model.

Zachary was last to be called. He was six years old and born with nonfunctioning legs below his knees. He sat in the front row, wearing a tiny tuxedo and scuffed leather kneepads, and was slated to have prostheses in the near future. Sliding off the metal folding chair, he posted on his right knee and swung his left knee forward before posting left and swinging right. By doing this over and over again, he slowly moved his three-

and-a-half-foot body towards the awards table. His smile, as bright as a full moon, seemed to fill his entire face, and his eyes shone like lighthouse beacons. He was an inspiration to all. Zachary was a crowd favorite.

The applause, hooting, and hollering competed with the band to give him the loudest accolade. As quick as a switch turns off a light, both the applause and the music were drowned out by primal, guttural screams from across the wall. The sounds echoed between the buildings and down the alleyway like a canyon. They seemed to fade out, only to be followed by louder and longer cries of anguish—and then another scream and another scream, like unwanted encores.

The family across the wall had just received word that one of the sisters who had gone to Port-au-Prince for supplies had been killed in the earthquake. She would be returned to La Gonâve tomorrow in a body bag for burial. Joy and sorrow were juxtaposed as life and death collided. It would happen again. The great intruder that was the earthquake had put an abrupt end to the celebration. More than before, it seemed imperative that we reevaluate our situation.

I went back to check with Don to see if he had any updates. He told me that the airport would not be open for commercial travel for weeks or months. The Hotel Montana had collapsed, killing everyone inside. Those people sitting poolside in the open, who had been swimming or having drinks, survived. The massive damage from the earthquake caused numerous deaths and injuries throughout the city.

That night, we ran the generator so that we could watch the news on the rabbit-eared TV in the rectory. We saw the newsreels of Port-au-Prince, with clouds of concrete dust hanging over the city, like a veil over a graveside mourner. It was time for us to get serious about our next steps. After Rose Emily's cell phone got some connection, she was able to have sporadic conversations with her husband. She got enough to let him know that we were all right but that we weren't sure how or when we would be able to leave. We had plenty of food and water, but, as one wry observer stated, we were running low on toilet paper and rum.

Through a combination of interrupted phone calls and networking back home, it was arranged for two ex-navy pilots who had access to a plane to land on the beach and rescue us. The surface of the beach would not be a problem, but the length needed to be adequate for them to land and taxi safely. As if walking the length of a long putt, we strode from one end to the other and measured it in yards. It seemed to be long enough. The next problems were that the flight would be arriving before dawn, while it was still dark out, and that the pickup needed to be accomplished with military precision. We were to be there at 6 a.m., ready to load.

Yet another problem was that the plane was only authorized to carry ten passengers and could not enter the United States with more than ten. Together, we planned a clandestine rendezvous and a secret stop for our overbooked plane. After the pickup, the former navy pilots could fly to the Turks and leave two of us there, who could then catch a commercial flight home. The rest could then enter the United States and go through customs at a small private airport without hassle. Fortunately, pilot pirates of the Caribbean could come to our rescue. In an instant, uncertainty had been converted to certainty, with generous doses of relief and excitement.

On Thursday, I visited Don again. He told me that this earthquake was starting to get personal for him. One of his Haitian assistants, who had spent all her money educating her children, had just learned that her daughter, an accountant, and her son, a law student, had both been crushed. In addition, he had heard bad news from a pastor friend of his in Port-au-Prince. Although his house had not been damaged, another pastor's church and school near the epicenter were gone, except for one classroom. There were many wounded lying around. He asked for help.

More big decisions loomed. When I next saw Don, he told me that he was going to send over supplies and people on Friday. The team would be comprised of Alison, a physician assistant who was halfway through her one-year-long mission assignment, and a couple of staff members. He asked if I could join them. I told him I would think about it. When I got back to our compound, I took Claire aside to talk everything through with her. I asked her to cover for me. I would have Claude drive me back up the mountain and bring medicines from the clinic pharmacy down to the hospital. I also told her that I was debating staying here and working at the hospital— or going with the Wesleyan team to see what we could do in Port-au-Prince. I had a new go or not to go.

That night at dinner, we planned to have everything packed before bed and ready for our flight out in the morning. The cooks would get up early and make coffee. Two trucks would be available to take all of us to the beach. Alarms were set for 5 a.m., in case anyone did fall asleep. Game on.

When the alarms sounded, most of us were already awake and active. Beams of light penetrated the darkness, hitting the floors and walls, as everyone dressed and took turns in the bathroom. It looked like a forensic search party or kids playing laser tag. But this was not just another game. This was not a flight to be missed. At 5:15 a.m., everyone was downstairs and ready. We had our coffee, loaded the trucks, and went to the airstrip.

Just as the first pink rays of morning sun peaked over the black mountaintops of mainland Haiti, we heard the engines and saw the blinking wing lights. The pilots circled and measured the landing strip, gauging their final approach. They came in low and touched down at the very beginning of the strip, using its full length to land, then turned around and taxied toward us. Since school had not started yet, thirty to forty children joined us in cheering its arrival. Before long, we started to load our bags.

It was time to tell them. I informed the group that I had decided to stay. This time, I would choose not to go. Claire immediately declared her approval. She knew she had no choice—but she supported the choice that I had made. They all understood my decision. The landing, the pickup, and the takeoff were done as efficiently as a NASCAR pit stop, slowed only by the delay caused by my hugging eleven people good-bye. The plane sped down the runway, cleared the soccer field, banked left, and circled back, and the pilot dipped his wings. I waved. My friends were on their way home.

CHAPTER 13

On the Go

There are defining moments in your life where you are uncertain about the future or your next step but unconcerned about the past. The past is the past, and these new moments redefine everything you ever thought you knew. Before Haiti, I was one person. After my experience in Haiti, I was another.

I had my work cut out for me. As soon as Claude and I got in the truck, his phone rang. I listened to him say, "Hullo... Okay..." and nothing else. Turning to me, he said, "Dr. Jim, you are needed at the hospital."

"What do they need?"

"They said something about a baby. I'm not sure."

"Okay, let's go."

We left the airstrip and returned to the hospital. Claude tapped the horn twice in front of the large iron gate to signal that we had arrived. The guard inside slid it open, allowing us to enter the courtyard. On a small table to the right, soaps, candies, and bottles of water and sodas were on display. It was a temporary gift shop.

Huddled near the hospital front door was a group of women, children, and one man. In the middle of the group was a pregnant woman. She sat on a stone ledge and rocked back and forth, stretching her hands over either side of her abdomen, as one would hold a basketball. Her fingertips tensed and relaxed in time with the uterine contractions that pulsated beneath them. Her breathing was short and rapid. Her eyes were closed tight. Her lips were stretched from side to side and were opened just enough to show her clenched teeth. When a contraction was at its peak, she bent forward and dipped her head between her knees. When the contraction relaxed, she would lean back, take a long deep breath, and look skyward, as if searching for some divine relief.

She was the one we had been called to see. She was the one who needed us.

She was unknown to us.

Claude spoke to her family and then relayed their message back to me. He told me, "Dr. Jim, she is in labor; her due date is today; she had a previous C-section."

I thought about how different my life looked in only one week's time. Last Friday, I had performed a repeat C-section with all the bells and whistles. A full and adoring family was present, happily anticipating the birth of a new child. To aid me, I had a full operating team, a full neonatal nursey team, and a full anesthesia team.

But today was different. A full family was once again present, but they were worried.

Many medical personnel were missing on account of the earthquake. Neither Dr. Martinez, the head surgeon, nor Nurse Francis, who administered the spinal anesthesia, was there. Both had gone to Port-au-Prince the day before to search for their children who lived there. A family practice physician, a surgical tech, and nurses were the only ones available to help.

I took the patient to an exam room. Her contractions were regular and strong. Her cervix was not dilated. The baby's heartbeat was good, but its head was very high. There was no chance of a vaginal delivery. In fact, there was an imminent chance of a ruptured uterus that would endanger both of their lives. The baby needed to be delivered—and now. I thought back to my residency training, when we occasionally discussed injecting a local anesthesia, like Novocain, into the surgical sites for an emergency C-section. We had never actually practiced it. But, in this case, it was the only option.

A lifetime of mottos raced through my mind. Boy Scouts: Be Prepared. High School: Ames Hi, Aims High. Fraternity: The True Gentleman Is Equal to All Emergencies. Medical School: Do No Harm.

With Claude translating, we explained the situation to the woman and her family. They agreed to proceed. In the OR, she lay on the table, anchored by a six-inch-wide rubber belt draped over her thighs. Her arms were fixed to arm boards with towels and had IV fluids running through them. She was prepped and draped in the usual sterile manner. So far, nothing was different from last Friday—except that she could still feel everything. A nurse sat on a stool at the head of the table, braced her forearms against its edge, placed her hands on the patient's cheekbones, wrapped her fingers under the patient's chin, and massaged the patient's temples with her thumbs. The nurse began to utter a low-pitched, guttural sound that resembled the relaxing tones from a cello or a French horn as the instruments' players warmed up. I seemed to sense vibrations coursing through the air, as well, and together they provided a calming influence for me.

I was hoping that she would put our patient into a trance before the surgery so that she would not feel the pain. As I filled the syringe with Novocain and prepared to infiltrate the skin, I suddenly remembered that an overdose of it could cause cardiac or central nervous system problems. I didn't remember the formula for maximum dosage. I was sweating beneath my surgical gown because of both the heat and my growing anxiety. I wished someone was massaging my head and chanting.

I injected sparingly under the scar of her previous incision, and there was no pain going through the skin, the fat, and the muscle layers. So far, so good. The peritoneum, or the large, baloonlike sac that houses the abdominal organs from the pelvis to the diaphragm, would be a challenge. So long as we could numb it, opening it would not be a problem. But tugging on it would stretch the upper part that was not numbed—and that would be painful for our patient. It did hurt. She let us know. She cried out, "Oh no." The words filled the room, and a translator was not needed. I felt the same way. The woman tried to lift her arms and legs and writhed from side to side. She became calmer with the increased cadence of the chanting and the firmer hand holding of the nurses. We paused for a moment to give her some additional relief.

The uterus was next. And it would be more difficult to deal with than last Friday's birth, when the little prince was delivered with ease and fanfare. This Friday, when I slid my hand around the baby's head, it was pinned by a massive contraction. Like a mountain man's spring-loaded trap captures his prey, my hand, wrist, and forearm were immobilized. This baby was big. Could this baby be delivered in between contractions so its head, shoulders, abdomen, or umbilical cord would not be squeezed, as well? This was going to be tough.

Apprehension added a third infusion of sweat to my already-soaked gown. One of the circulating nurses wiped my dripping brow. We waited for the contraction to relax and prepared to lift the baby up and out before the next one. Neither the mother nor I were interested in being there any longer than was necessary. *Let's make it one and done,* I thought to myself.

With a combination of me lifting the head from below, my assistant applying fundal pressure from above, and all of us filling the air with grunts, groans, and chants, we delivered a broad-shouldered, compact, nine-pound baby boy. Nine pounds is large by American standards and huge by Haitian standards. The baby cried, and his eyes blinked. His mother sighed, her eyes filled with relief. The nurses uttered a cheer—and their eyes sparkled with joy in the process. I was silent and closed mine for a second. We did it. Closing the tissue layers was painless and went well. The woman had no ill effects from the Novocain and was soon cradling her precious little prince.

At two o'clock, it was time to leave La Gonâve and go to Port-au-Prince. I made one last check on the mother and her baby before we left. She had little pain and was eating beans and rice, which her family had brought her. Her son was ready to nurse. Once again, a mother who had just been through an ordeal and deserved full attention forwent her own needs and wished me, "Bon chance." She was grateful. I was grateful that I had been able to help her—and to have met her.

We loaded the truck with our supplies and headed to the dock. A lobster boat from Nova Scotia that had recently been donated to the Wesleyans was moored there. It had a pilot's cabin in front and plenty of room on the deck for the supplies and us. It would be sturdy on the sea. We backed the truck up to the edge of the dock, where cleats held the tightly tethered rope of the boat. A multitude of volunteer dockwork-ers greeted us on arrival. Most wore jeans, tennis shoes, and very tight-fitted T-shirts. They were proud of their iron man physiques. Some wore baseball hats, extolling an NCAA foot-ball team as National Champions. It was, however, the losing team's hats that had been donated to the island.

With the expertise of air traffic controllers, they simultane-ously facilitated the loading of our cargo and directed boats in and out of the canal. Specifically, they helped the boats avoid entangling the anchor lines of other docked vessels. Shouting and waving, they empathically directed a slow-moving boat to dock next to us. The engine barely made a sound. The crews balanced themselves on the boat's side rails and were strangely quiet. A large, black tarp covered the cargo, which filled the entire hold at its base and which rose to central peak from fore to aft. It looked like a graceful black swan coming home. It came alongside our vessel, and the mooring ropes were secured. This boat usually carried bags of charcoal.

The tarp was removed. When we saw the cargo, we stood motionless and were silent. Inside the boat, shiny, black body bags, each with a single, white tag attached to the zipper grommet, were neatly stacked like logs. The adult-sized bags formed the base and angled up like the side of a pyramid. The child-sized ones rested on top. The child-sized bags were the first to be lifted down, carried to the bow, and gently handed across the water to the dock crew. They were placed on the ground next to the waiting pickup trucks. After the adults were placed on the truck beds, they could rest on top again. Everyone would be delivered to his or her family for burial.

We went back to loading our medical supplies without speaking. This was no longer the usual goodwill mission trip. Once again, life and death were juxtaposed.

Casting off from the dock, we were not as careful as the black swan boat had been on arriving. As we headed out, our propeller snagged on another boat's stretched anchor line and stopped our progress, and it was like being stuck in weeds in the shallows on a fishing trip. The captain tried going back and forth to disentangle it, but he was unsuccessful. Two fit young men quickly put on goggles and dove into the water. The anchor rope was as taught as a circus high wire. The anchor was too deep and heavy to be lifted in order to provide enough slack to unwind the rope from the blades. After three attempts, the captain handed the young men a machete and commanded them to cut it. They did. The lower portion slipped from the blades, and the upper portion floated up limp to the surface. I thought we were going to be in trouble. The captain gunned the engine.

We were off. Someone else would have to deal with the anchorless captain. For the next thirty minutes, the bow of the boat cut through the calm, sapphire-blue sea, its wake shooting shimmering eighteen-carat droplets out of its white, turbulent wake and into the fresh air. As we crossed the bay, we could see the US Naval ships with their gunmetal grey silhouettes and tall conning towers patrolling and monitoring the marine traffic. It reminded me of scenes from a World War II documentary.

Docking at our destination presented its own challenges. Normally, a boat could come alongside the concrete pier to be stabilized and unloaded. Since it was low tide, the water depth was too shallow along the pier. Between that and the rocky shoreline, we could not dock. We could only maintain buoyancy two or three feet from the end of the pier, where there were no cleats to secure the ropes.

Pastor Jacob, another new best Haitian friend, was in

charge of the land crew. He motioned for us to toss the rope ends to two men who grabbed them. While they engaged in a tug of war with the sea to keep us close to the pier, we heaved boxes over the bow, trying to time the tosses with the height of the incoming waves. As we heaved the boxes, we were faced with the addition challenge of not slipping and falling into the drink or losing the cargo. The catcher, meanwhile, had to make sure the cargo did not break on the concrete dock. Our own leaps, a combination of standing vertical and long-jumping from boat to dock, required an extra shot of adrenaline. I felt as if I had just had a quadruple espresso. If this wasn't so serious, it could have been a new Olympic sport or an American Ninja Warriors challenge.

Once we were all safely on land and settled, we loaded Pastor Jacob's white, four-door Toyota pickup truck. On his truck, an iron cage extended from the bed to two feet above the rooftop, with a door at the rear. After we crammed the supplies into the truck, Pastor Jacob padlocked the door. Ready to get moving, we squeezed three into the front seat and four into the back. We were off. It was all go again.

CHAPTER 14

Back to Port-au-Prince

The trip to Port-au-Prince was familiar but different. The first evidence of destruction was the jagged cracks in the country road. As we approached the small town of Cabaret, we saw that collapsed walls and roofs of homes had spilled onto the street. In front of us, a utility pole had hammered a small yellow bus into the ground and lay across its hood. With its crumpled fender and flattened right front tire, it resembled a horse with a broken leg bowing on its front quarter.

Travel was slow. Pastor Jacob told us it would get worse. People were milling about, talking with one another, and poking through the crumbled debris. Somehow, multiple small, open-air fruit and vegetable stands had survived. Pastor Jacob stopped to buy bananas and melons. He also procured three one-gallon plastic jugs filled with gasoline. Supplies were very slim in Port-au-Prince, so we were lucky to get even this much.

Farther down the road, we came upon a slow-moving pickup truck headed to town. As we approached, we saw five young men sitting on bags of rice with their legs hanging over the sides of the truck. When we got closer, we noticed an elderly woman who was covered by a yellow bedsheet and lying in the center of the bags. One of the boys held an umbrella to shade her dry, wrinkled face. Another held a bag of IV fluids that was infusing into her left forearm. We came alongside and signaled for them to stop. The boys told us that a falling cinder block had gouged the woman's skin, exposing the muscle beneath. This makeshift ambulance and crew were taking her to Port-au-Prince, hoping to find care for her.

She did not look well. She was nauseated was twisting a rag with her gnarled fingers as she tried to relieve the pain. Under the sheet, we saw crimson-soaked gauze wrapped around her right thigh. There was nothing we could do for the injury except clean and redress the raw tissue. We gave her fresh gauze and paper tape, some pain pills, an anti-nausea wafer, and antibiotics. This was our first introduction to MacGyver medicine.

Our group squeezed back into the seats and headed to town. I became apprehensive. Did we have enough supplies— or the proper supplies—for this kind of battlefield medicine? Would my medical practice, which was so specialized, be adequate for the tasks ahead? I began to try to recall lessons from medical school rotations and emergency room stints from forty years ago that would be more useful than the obstetrics that I practiced every day in my profession.

When we approached the city limits, we were confronted by the full extent of the destruction and devastation. It was ready for us, but were we ready for it? The scene was grim. Homes built on the hillsides had cascaded down on top of each other like dominoes. Multistoried buildings on flat ground had fallen straight down, their collapsed floors resembling stacks of pancakes. Anything and anyone between those floors would have been crushed, as if in a trash compactor. Later, we would learn that cinderblocks under extreme pressure could be hurled from the walls like missiles or cannonballs, inflicting further harm on unsuspecting targets.

Pastor Jacob said he would take us on a tour before we went to his home. Cement dust covered everything and seemed a strange unifying factor. In the central city, cars were crushed, pinned down by cinder blocks and telephone poles. The crumpled buildings that hadn't been flattened looked like small mountains with crevasses and jagged edges of rock jutting upward.

A woman wearing flip-flops, a denim skirt, and a dirt-smudged white blouse was climbing up and down and around one of these newly formed ruins. Like a rock climber, she tested handholds and footholds, making sure they were stable before shifting her body to a new position. Like many others out in the debris, she covered her nose and mouth with a bandana or surgical mask to keep the dust and the nauseating stench of decaying bodies buried in the rubble from overwhelming her. I imagined that the bandana's inward and outward movement, like a bellows, gave reassurance that she was still alive with every breath. It also provided a barrier from the reality of agony, as she peered into the darkness between slabs of concrete.

What was she looking for? Maybe she was looking for evidence of a loved one or hoping to hear the sound of a shout, a cry, or a whimper. Maybe she was looking for a remnant of her possessions that may have escaped damage. Something. Anything.

All around us, people were trying to make the best of a dire situation. Across the street and extending for many blocks in both directions, we could see sticks and metal poles propping up blue tarp roofs. People draped sheets or blankets on the sides to get some privacy. In the open, central areas of dust and grass, we spotted large cauldrons filled with water, onions, a variety of scarce vegetables, and spices simmering over charcoal fires. The secret ingredient dropped into the mixture was a whole scotch bonnet pepper. With cloves that had been poked through and that covered its entire surface, it resembled an underwater mine. The aroma of Creole cooking competed with the stench—and, for the moment, won.

The whole scene reminded me of a gigantic Grateful Dead village. Women squatted and tended to the fires, men patrolled and offered aid to anyone, and children with wide, unblinking eyes looked for a hand to hold. Unlike with the Grateful Dead, there was no music. They still needed a miracle.

Carefully, we weaved our way into the center of the city. The Presidential Palace, an all-white building with central columns at its entry and three domes (one central and one at each end) used to stand majestically. The shifting earth had taken down one end. Now, the palace looked like an ocean liner that was listing and about to sink. Not far away, the Catholic and Episcopal cathedrals had collapsed, except for a few remaining columns and half walls. The destruction was massive and indiscriminate.

The sunlight was fading, and darkness was creeping into the city. Pastel shades of pink, red, and orange splashed across the gray-and-white rubble on one side of a mound and contrasted with shadows on the other side. This palette of light and dark strangely reminded me of a low winter sun splashing its setting rays across the sand dunes of the Florida panhandle. From a mound near the cathedrals, a lone dove ascended and circled before flying away. Maybe there was a miracle out there somewhere.

It was time for our tour to end and travel to Pastor Jacob's home in Delmas, a part of the city that was relatively undamaged. The streets in his neighborhood were narrow but had no debris. At the end of a street, we stopped in front of another large metal gate. Pastor Jacob honked his horn with two quick taps. His ten-year-old son slid the gate open, and we entered the courtyard. His wife and eight-year-old daughter welcomed us at the front door with hugs and invited us inside. After this long day, it felt good to stretch out and sit for a while.

The house had been built as a guesthouse. A large table that could seat twelve or more divided the kitchen from a sparse but functional great room, which we would later we use to organize our medicines and supplies. The living room was spacious, with only a few chairs and an L-shaped couch. There, we had plenty of room to put suitcases, backpacks, duffle bags, or any other large items that we needed to store. A card table in the corner served as a desk. We had everything we needed.

They had a small generator that they used intermittently to provide just enough electricity to keep the refrigerator cool and to power cell phone and computer chargers that were scattered on the card table with their cords hanging over the side It reminded me of the legs of the young men hanging over the pickup truck. I wondered if they had found help for their patient.

Upstairs, the bedrooms were dormitory-style, with a dozen metal-framed bunk beds in each room. Each bed was fitted with a fresh and unwrinkled set of sheets. The window openings were covered with screens. The entire setup reminded me of the cold-air dorm of my fraternity. Because of fire codes and health concerns in those crowded conditions, the windows had to remain open, even in the winter months. On occasion, one might wake up covered with snow. This, however, was a warm-air dorm, so we did not have to worry about that.

Our original plan was to spend the next day organizing for a trip to Petite-Goâve, which sits on a small bay several miles away from Port-au-Prince. Some of the filming of *Pirates of the Caribbean* supposedly happened there. Contrary to the movie, our Petite-Goâve had an old church camp and little else. The people were essentially isolated. As a result, we planned to establish a mobile triage clinic until more sophisticated operations arrived. An expat caretaker lived at Petite-Goâve and had assembled a skeleton crew of cooks and handymen who would be able to facilitate our visit. It, like the house we were currently in, also had warm-air dorms.

During dinner of black bean soup, fresh banana-and-melon salad, and flatbread, Pastor Jacob informed us that there was a change of plan for tomorrow. Instead of organizing ourselves, we would instead go to Carrefour, an area of the city where some of the worst damage was. One of his pastor friends, whose church and school had been destroyed except for one classroom, had asked for our help for at least a day. He told him many injured individuals were lying on the open ground, waiting for help. Once again, the question presented itself: To go or not to go? We had not planned on this detour. Nevertheless, we decided to go to Carrefour.

That night was hot and still. The heat, as well as worrying about tomorrow's clinic, made it difficult for me to sleep. I had heard about yogis who could change their body temperatures by engaging their mental states. I tried to imagine that I was in my cold-air dorm, with a blast of northern air circulating. That did not work. I then imagined I was breathing in air that passed over a giant block of ice and disseminating it through my lungs to the tiniest of peripheral blood vessels on my face and chest to give myself a cold flash, so to speak. That did not work. I remained restless.

Finally, at 6 a.m., the sun came up and I got up. I had a cup of hot coffee, which seemed to get things back in balance. After a breakfast of oatmeal and toast, we prepared to go to Carrefour. Dressed in our blue scrubs, we loaded our medicines, sutures, bandages, orthopedic casting materials, and a case of bottled water into the caged truck bed. We covered everything with blankets to prevent potential looters from getting too interested in the supplies that we were carrying with us.

Like a beginner in driving school negotiating a chicane of orange cones, Pastor Jacob navigated the maze of debris, flattened cars, trucks, and small fires in the streets as we traveled to the school and the church. The morning was eerily quiet. The roosters were not crowing. The usual symphony of horns from darting motorcycles, sputtering car engines, and large trucks lumbering on the streets was strangely absent. It reminded me of my visit to Ground Zero, one month after that tragedy. It was reverential and ghostlike, all at the same time.

Carrefour is built on a hillside, with switchback roads. The collapsed houses that were piled on top of one another like rockslides or slag heaps blocked some of these roads. In every direction, Carrefour looked like the cities in Europe that had been mercilessly bombed during World War II. We had to detour several times.

As we approached our destination, a new obstacle appeared. Many survivors were now living, cooking, and sleeping on the street in makeshift communities, the result of homelessness or the fear of more buildings collapsing because of aftershocks. They were trying to get as far away as possible from the danger. Some of the survivors had mattresses to lie on, while others had blankets. Children around them rested on adults who may or may not have been relatives. All around them, they had piled up the remnants of fallen walls to act as speed bumps or barriers. They were using the debris to try to protect their new squatter domains. We had to be extra careful not to run into anything or anyone as we maneuvered through the obstacle course.

I began to question myself again. I thought, *I know am looking at all of this with my eyes, but am I really seeing anything? Even though I can hear you, am I really listening to what you say? Can I really comprehend the extent of this devastation? Do I really know what it means to lose your personal records, possessions, family, or limb?* It is one thing to see a wound, categorize it as something that needs to be fixed, and fix it. It is another thing to know the wound yourself and have to live with it. My stomach tightened into a knot, my mouth went dry, and my mind overwhelmed as I observed these disheveled, dust-covered, and hungry street people, grieving their losses and thirsting for help.

Just ahead on the right, I saw an opening in a wall, which was the entrance to the church and the schoolyard. We were about to turn in and escape this area of desperation when there was a knock on Pastor Jacob's window. One of the street people, a man with callused hands, swollen knuckles, and fingers that were slightly bent from grasping a machete was the one who sought our attention. Pastor Jacob stopped and rolled down his window. The man bent forward. His cheeks were wrinkled from the sun, and his lips were parched. His curly, black beard was laced with gray, and his cataracts were thick. On top of his head, a Rasta cap with red, green, yellow, and black colors in a sawtooth pattern housed his dreadlocks.

His presence filled the window like a TV close-up. He asked, "Do you have any water?"

Pastor Jacob was firm and gentle, but answered, "No." The man backed up like a camera fade away, turned, and departed.

But wait! We did have water hidden beneath our supplies. I wanted to ask Pastor Jacob, "Aren't we Christians or humanitarians who should share and care for others? Surely, we can spare a bottle. I'm sure he would probably share it with others. I've seen that before with the candy. He might have used it to make soup." Then, it dawned on me. Like on an airplane, we are supposed to secure our own oxygen masks before helping others. We should first keep the water for ourselves, and then we can tend to the needs of others. How could I have been so quick to judge Pastor Jacob's refusal of the request?

Pastor Jacob closed his window and drove through the opening in the wall. He parked the truck, and we got out to survey the surroundings. The church had been leveled to the ground; the school had crumbled, except for one classroom. In the yard, we spotted forty or fifty injured patients sporting rags or bandanas as bandages around their legs, arms, or heads. Many lay on the ground. Some sat on piles of cinder blocks, while others leaned against each other, holding their children on their laps. We knew more would come. The work ahead of us seemed daunting.

They had already established a triage system, where the patients would each wait their turn. One girl, who was about twelve years old, had been placed nearest the classroom door. She was first in line. She lay on a makeshift stretcher comprised of a blanket stretched between two rebar poles. Two boards splinted her right leg. It was bent midthigh. The last time I had fixed a broken femur was ... never. I asked Alison, who was a physician assistant, if she knew what to do. She cocked her head, arched her right eyebrow, and nodded yes.

We began to organize before starting treatments. The cinder block room was painted green, and it was windowless. All in all, it measured about thirty by thirty-six feet. The only source of ventilation was an eight-to-twelve-inch gap between the roof and the walls. Spotting tables placed against the back wall and part of one sidewall, we chose to organize our various supplies there. Medicines, bandages, sutures, and instruments were in their own places. Wooden grade school chairs and folded-up lawn chairs that could be extended to bed length provided centers for patient care.

Two adult women and two men who were probably in their early twenties were waiting for us. They knew enough English to offer their services as translators. We immediately accepted their offer and thanked them. They took great pride in being part of the team. In spite of the heat and crowded quarters, they remained calm and cool. One of the boys, Jean Louis, wore a robin's-egg blue scarf looped around his neck like a Frenchman strolling along the Seine. He quickly became my right-hand man and seemed to relish his newfound status.

It was time to set the fracture. Alison explained that we would bring the girl in on her stretcher, keeping her flat on her back with her legs together. The splinted leg would be shorter when laid parallel to the other. We would have to stretch it out to make the legs of equal length. This would set the broken ends of the bone in close proximity. Next, we would place a rolled-up towel under the knee to provide a small bend before casting. Once the cast material hardened, the girl would be stable enough to travel to one of the more sophisticated trauma centers being established by Doctors Without Borders or other countries for further evaluation and care. The girl was stoic during the procedure, exhaling a long sigh of relief when it was finally done. She thanked us with a soft handshake.

When it was their turn, friends and family members who had been waiting began to bring their loved ones inside. Most of the injuries were abrasions, deep gashes, lacerations, and fractures. Dirt, threads of clothes, and small bits of concrete had to be removed from the skinless areas before we could apply ointments and bandages or suture those that had skin. We used betadine, hydrogen peroxide, and some of our water to wash away the loose and superficial foreign bodies before picking out the deeper ones. Eventually, we trained our translators to clean the wounds before we did the suturing in order to expedite the care and see everyone. Our day would not end until dusk.

The combination of the warm air, our heightened body temperatures, and the lack of circulation in the small, crowded room turned it into an unwelcome sauna. We had been cleaning wounds, suturing lacerations, and stabilizing fractures for several hours. I sat on a chair with my back to the door, treating a man who lay on one of the extended lawn chairs in front of me. We cleaned and applied antibiotic ointments to his extensive facial, arm, and leg injuries. Though he had many wounds, they were not too severe. Jean Louis, the Frenchman, translator, and now first assistant, deftly wrapped the gauze dressing over them all. Our patient managed a crooked grin, rose from the treatment table, steadied himself, and began to lurch with a stiff-legged gait. He looked like a half-dressed mummy ready for Halloween or a movie audition. As he walked out of the room, we wished him, "Bon chance."

By this time, we were hot and thirsty. I turned towards the door, hoping to catch a bit of breeze coming through and wanting to see who was coming in next. Standing there in stillness and filling the entire doorway was the street man we had previously encountered. His shirt and pants were torn, and he was barefooted. In each of his long, muscular arms, he cradled five or six bottles of water. He squatted, placed them on the floor, and said, "You will need these." Just as before, he backed away, turned, and departed. I was struck once again by the thoughtfulness and generosity of the street people, along with my continued misconceptions about them.

We continued our work until it was almost dusk. When it was quitting time, Pastor Jacob, who had been running errands, suddenly burst through door, shouting, "You need to save this man."

He had a tight grasp on his upper arm and brought him in to see us. Blood was streaming down his face and covered his chest. Great. Just like at home. Oftentimes, the last patient is the most in need.

We asked the man what had happened. He told us, "I was just walking along the street, having survived the earthquake. And then, I was nearly killed by an iron cage bouncing off his truck."

Pastor Jacob told us that when he was nearly here to pick us up, he unknowingly drove under a low-hanging telephone wire, which had scraped the roof of the cab. After that, it had caught the front of the cage, ripping it out of the back bed, and sending it cartwheeling towards its victim. The man had been injured by our cab.

Jean Louis, who was now nearly advanced to the level of a licensed ER assistant, calmed the man down and told him that we would be able to fix everything. Jean Louis deftly wiped the blood from his forehead and face. The man had a semilunar laceration of his entire front scalp along his hairline that was not too detached from his skull. It was also clean. Jean Louis applied firm pressure to the injury with his gloved hands to stop the bleeding. He had the appearance of an officiate laying hands on someone during an initiation ceremony. Once the bleeding was controlled, we quickly approximated the skin edges with our last surgical stapler. In seven to ten days, the man or a friend could use the staple remover we had given him to take the staples out. Free to go, the man now sported a rather roguish look. Hopefully, he would tell his friends a more daring story than what had actually happened.

I went outside the wall and looked for the man in the Rasta cap, the water man. Like a hero in a movie, he was gone by the final scene. I missed him. I missed not being able to thank him, commend him, or tell him that I would not forget him. I missed not being able to shake his hand. I wondered if I would ever see him again.

We loaded the cageless truck with what was left of our supplies and headed home. As the sunlight faded, the darkness transformed the jagged piles of rubble into smooth mounds of gray and black so that it looked like a thousand sea turtles headed down the hill and back to the ocean.

Pastor Jacob had been to the airport while we were working and had picked up a group of volunteers from Scotland. In the past, they had worked with him and Don to finance and build new medical facilities on La Gonâve. Ever ready to help, they had wasted no time in responding to the crisis. After he met them at the airport, Jacob had taken them and ten large duffle bags full of more medical supplies to his home. Jacob had also learned three physicians and more supplies were coming from the Midwest tomorrow. He began to opine that we would need more vehicles for the trip to Petite-Goâve. Under the current circumstances, all the car rental businesses were going to be

closed for a while—and we had not seen many viable candidates on the streets. We would have to come up with a different plan.

The farther we drove, the darker it got. Soon it was as if
we were navigating a cave with our headlights sending a lim-
ited shaft of light ahead like a beam from a headlamp. Since
we were descending a hill, Pastor Jacob was using the brakes
more than the gas. Suddenly, near the bottom, he floored the
accelerator. He started honking, weaving in and out of traffic
like a NASCAR driver or a lioness on the hunt.

The day had been long. I was tired and a bit irritable. I
yelled, "What are you doing?" He said he had seen a truck.
Now, he was more like the lioness on a hunt. We took a
tight turn around a corner and all slid to the right as the car
whipped around the bend. Two blocks ahead of us was a moving van, twenty-four feet in length. It had wooden sidewalls
and a roof, but the back end was open. Pastor Jacob gunned
the engine, honked, and waved as he cut across the prey's left-
front fender. As he zoomed in front of him, the other driver
pulled to the curb and slammed on his brakes.

The truck driver was now honking, waving, and shouting.
Pastor Jacob jumped out and ran to his window. Now, they
were both waving and shouting. Other cars around us took
over the honking. After a few minutes, Pastor Jacob got back
in the car, and we headed home. He explained that he had
negotiated for the use of the truck for tomorrow's trip. The
truck owner and his sidekick would meet us at the airport,
where we would pick up the incoming crew and supplies.
From there, we would drive to Petite-Goâve. Pastor Jacob had
given them only a few Haitian dollars to secure the deal. I was
amazed at how two strangers trusted each other with little
more than each other's word, and that both the truck and the

full amount of money would be ready for exchange.

When we got home, the crew from Scotland greeted us with handshakes, hugs, and, "How you doin' mate?" In addition to the medical supplies, they had brought a twenty-five-year-old single malt scotch, which they had already opened and were ready to share. That night, the hot-air dorm felt just right.

CHAPTER 15

Journey to the Sea

The morning crept in with its new quietness, simultaneously serene and spooky, like a serpent slithering in the grass. I didn't know whether it would bring danger and adversity to our path or would just move on without incident.

After a breakfast of coffee, fruit, and oatmeal, we loaded the new supply bags into the cageless truck. I saw Justin give Don a six-inch stack of bills. It looked like US currency, but the denominations were not visible. Cash was definitely king in these circumstances. From what I could tell, it appeared to be a lot of money. Don then gave some to Pastor Jacob so that he would be able to pay the truck driver.

We drove to the airport and found the driver parked next to a UN tank manned with soldiers wearing black boots, green fatigues, bulletproof vests, and robin's-egg blue helmets. Sitting on top of the tank, they guarded the entrance to the tarmac. We transferred our bags to his truck and then spoke to the machine gun toting guards. We explained that our mission was to pick up more supplies and physicians who would be flying in from the States on a Gulfstream jet, courtesy of a major corporation. Satisfied with our story, the soldiers let us drive through the razor-wired fence. The shattered windows and cracked walls of the main terminal made it look like a block of ice that had had hot water poured over it. It was not operational.

Once again, we would have to improvise. We drove a short distance to an area filled with jeeps with machine guns mounted on them. We parked between the jeeps and got out. A few yards away, we noticed a flatbed truck with five layers of brand new portable Honda generators. There were 250 of them, and one of them would be a perfect addition for our mission. Surely, they could spare one.

We asked one of the Brazilian guards if we could take one for our medical efforts. He either did not understand us or chose not to understand us. He waved us off with his machine gun and a scowl. I flashed back to my shoplifting days, when our juvenile gang could easily slide a magazine under our T-shirts or pocket a pack of gum and leave the store. Eventually, we got caught and were penalized by our parents. But the stakes were higher this time. The consequences of attempting this heist just might be a bit more severe than not receiving a Little League championship trophy. We realized that it would not be a prudent endeavor to try to steal one.

We moved away and walked onto the edge of the tarmac. Usually, there were only a few commercial airplanes and some baggage carts out on the tarmac. This time, the tarmac was a combination of an air show jammed with everything from small, single-engine planes to gigantic transport planes, and an open-air market where pallets of water, food, and clothes were unloaded. Haitian police were supervising the entire operation. Dressed in berets, khaki shirts with patches on the shoulders and ribbons on the front pockets, wide, black belts that held the holster for a pistol and a strap for a billy club, and dark blue pants with a red stripe running down to their shiny black boots, they were an imposing sight.

We made our way to an open area to look for our plane among the incoming flights. All we knew was that it had turned-up wing tips and a blue mark on the tail. A US Air Force colonel, who seemed to be of some importance, approached us and asked what we were doing there. Our blue scrubs enhanced our credibility that we were doctors and explained our presence. The colonel then offered to take us over to a domed tent with industrial-sized generators and rotating radar screens set up near the runway. He said he could help us make our connection. The colonel's upright posture and measured stride reflected the pride he had in leading this field trip. We were proud to see how our finest service men and women ran their show—and relieved to know when our flight was landing. There, we got to see firsthand a mobile air-traffic control center that had been developed for use during the desert wars. Now it served a humanitarian cause.

Our tour was shortened when the colonel was called to attend to something more urgent and had to abandon us. Before he left, we asked if he could help us get one of the generators we had previously failed to obtain. He shrugged his shoulders, hung his arms palms forward, and gave a slight grimace.

Dr. Bill would not take no for an answer again so easily. He asked the colonel where he was from. "Brooklyn," the colonel replied.

"Tell me, if that truck was parked in Brooklyn, how many generators do you think would vanish before the delivery was accomplished?" Dr. Bill asked.

Colonel Burke stopped in his tracks. Turning towards the guards, he whistled, waved, and shouted something in Portuguese as he pointed at us. The guards immediately hopped off the truck, slung their weapons onto their back, grabbed two generators, and put them into our truck.

Blue scrubs and blue helmets faced each other under a blue sky. Sacré bleu. We did our best rendition of a salute *M*A*S*H*-style. No one questioned us again. We thanked the colonel and turned our attention back to the tarmac. In addition to the planes landing there, several were taking off. Some were headed back to get more supplies, but the largest, most impressive planes were preparing to transport evacuees to Florida. They had been processed the day before through our embassy, which had looked like a ticket booth selling tickets to a Rolling Stone concert or a parking lot filled with Black Friday shoppers, waiting for the doors to open.

We saw our plane land and taxi to an open spot. The door popped open and Dr. Tom, a family physician, and Dr. Bob, a surgeon, descended. The pilot came down and opened the luggage compartment so that we could unload several boxes and duffle bags of supplies they had obtained from the hospital. Haitian personnel came over with flatbed carts and helped us take it all to the rented truck. It was easy to throw the bags into the open back end. It reminded me of throwing bales of hay onto a farm trailer. And there was still plenty of room for us in the truck. One could stand up inside the truck or sit on a full-length bench on either side.

Once we secured the generators and all the other supplies in the rented truck, we were ready for the next stop. We headed for a warehouse, where there were more supplies. Dr. Kate would be there to join us. Dr. Kate had been practicing general medicine in Haiti for several years. Her knowledge of the culture and her excellent Creole language skills would be invaluable. After everything was loaded, Pastor Jacob got in his truck to lead the way. We were off, headed to Petite-Goâve in our large, open-ended truck, with two drivers whom we had just met. Once again, we were putting our trust in the skills and goodwill of the Haitian people.

Like hitchhiking in college, the mixture of adventure and trepidation kept all of us on high alert. The ten of us in the back of the truck had a slight idea of where we were going and that we needed this transportation. We trusted that we weren't being totally irresponsible by putting our fate in the hands of strangers. During the ride, we found it more comfortable to lounge on the supply bags than to sit on the narrow benches, and we took a moment to relax.

The trip through Port-au-Prince was smooth. It was still a city in chaos, but it was beginning to function. On the far edge of town, some gas stations remained intact and open. The lines for gasoline were long, extending from the pumps, across the parking area, and down the shoulder of the road for several hundred yards. A mixture of cars, trucks, motorcycles, and individuals with gallon plastic jugs queued for fuel. The people outnumbered the vehicles about twenty to one. Everyone remained patient and orderly, awaiting their fuel ration. It was a marked contrast from newsreels showing people throwing rocks and stealing food in times of shortage.

Once we were in the countryside, the fresh, salty air refreshed our skin and cleansed our lungs of the dust of the crumbled city. To the right of the road stood the sea. To the left stood the mountains. The road seemed to have a life of its own, winding off from its straight path into hills. It was cracked in many places. Some cracks were only a few inches wide, others nearly a foot wide—some extended from shoulder to shoulder. We had another maze to navigate.

Any time we approached a wide crack, our driver, Paul, would slow down and creep across the split in the road. To make up time, he would speed on unimpaired flat stretches of road. Going up hills was like mountain climbing, slow and steady. Going down was like being on a rollercoaster or skiing a black run, freewheeling with an occasional lean to the left or right. It reminded me of the wild descent into Las Vegas many years ago. Driving down those hills was the only time I was apprehensive. I wondered when Paul or whoever owned this truck had last had a safety inspection. There had probably never been one.

To distract myself, I listened for failing brakes or a blown-out tire. I was prepared to jump out if we tipped and somehow cascaded into a ravine. Not that I would be able to perform any lifesaving maneuver in that situation, but keeping an ear out was a better alternative to thinking about how we would be tossed around with boxes, bags, and each other like rocks in a tumbler. It also kept me focused. Fortunately, no emergencies occurred. After two hours, we stopped on a flat stretch of road. To the right of us was a path through tall grass that led to an open, rusted gate. We drove inside and parked, having at last made it to our destination.

This was the campground. All around us, picnic tables were scattered among the mango trees and spread around the yard without any pattern. On the right was a white bungalow where Roger, the caretaker, lived. The paint of his bungalow was peeling, and the porch was sagging like a disheveled actor shedding his makeup and bent with age. On the left was a long, one-story building with yellow cinderblock walls and a rusted tin roof. A door in the center of the building opened into a hallway that led to the other side. A few feet inside the building, two, thick, wooden doors stood across from each other. The skeleton of the building was a sturdy metal frame. Through each door, we found two rows of metal bunk beds. The room to the right was for women and the one to the left for men. Several yards away and near the beach stood cement latrines, christened with tin doors and wooden latches.

Standing on the northwestern edge of the property above the beach, I saw quite a sight. To the right, there was open water. To the left, the land continued in an arc that ended straight ahead and about a half mile out. The beachfront was a part of a semicircular cove that provided a safe harbor. As I looked beyond the beach, I could imagine Blackbeard or Jack Sparrow anchoring their pirate galleons here, either for safety or in hiding. This was prime real estate. It was ironic to consider that the same natural forces of shifting rocks or tectonic plates that had created this pristine setting now had caused destruction and chaos.

The front door of the bungalow creaked open, and Roger appeared. Roger stood about five feet, six inches, with a stout combination of muscle and belly. His most prominent feature, a full red beard, covered his cheeks and hid his mouth. Roger wore a short-sleeved island shirt with red-hibiscus-and-green-cattail prints on a white background, which hung over his beltless cargo shorts. He carried a satellite phone in his left hand and palmed a cigarette in his right. He could have passed for a descendant of one of those ancient mariners or an expat reliving his hippie days. He spoke very little and remained mysterious. At any rate, he would be the boss man.

At his direction, several boys and men came to the truck and transferred the contents to the dormitories. As we were unloading, a stout woman wearing silver flip-flops that contrasted well with her crimson toenail polish, a full milk-chocolate-colored skirt, and a salmon-colored tank top that fit tightly around her ample chest approached us. Though she was top heavy, her gait was agile. Her skin was the color of dark chocolate, and her fleshy cheeks looked like giant truffles. This was Madame Madeline, our cook. Her eyes looked straight through me and conveyed nothing. I couldn't tell if she was in shock or had seen this before. Perhaps she was skeptical, waiting to see if we could really do any good. I wondered the same thing.

Shortly afterward, a young man of about eighteen came to shake my hand and told me, "I am Jonas. I am a translator." I was amazed at his confidence and the pride he took in his appearance. His long-sleeved blue shirt and khaki pants were pressed, and his dark brown shoes were polished. I liked his selection. I had seen the irons used to press clothes or tablecloths. Pressing clothes with these is a big ordeal. The irons are heavy, thick, anvil-shaped instruments with a smooth, flat bottom and a hollowed-out cavity where hot charcoal is placed. A plate covers the embers, which prevents them from falling out or burning one's hand, and the handle arcs over it. I thought of Jonas ironing his clothes with one every morning.

I introduced myself to Jonas and thanked him for being there. He said he would like English lessons in return for his services. I agreed. What better bargain could there be than to share our languages, our cultures, our respect, and our commitment to help? We had a lot to share with each other. This arrangement seemed as if it had more potential to build relationships than subsidies, embargoes, or handouts. I relished the chance to be a part of such relationship building.

It was time to get to work. First, we organized all of our materials in the dorms. Next, we began to build our combination acute care, emergency room, and surgical suites facility. We placed white plastic chairs out in the yard for a waiting room. We used a long table to separate them from the place where we would set up stations for setting fractures, cleaning wounds, and suturing minor lacerations. The long table would also serve as a triage center. We secured a ten-foot edge of blue tarp to a rebar sticking up out of a security wall, and we tethered the other corners to nearby tree branches. We extended another tarp from the wall of the dormitory to bunk beds that had been brought outside. Finally, we placed long folding tables underneath the tarps to serve as our operating rooms. The entire operation was a combination of a *M*A*S*H* unit and *Field of Dreams*. Build it, and they would come.

Off to the side, I heard the sound of wood being chopped. Four men had dug four postholes with their machetes, making a twelve-foot square. They placed posts seven feet tall and eight inches in diameter that were made from tree trunks into the postholes. They had notched the tops of the tree trunks and with rope secured smaller branches as crossbeams from corner to corner. On top from side to side they crisscrossed more branches and covered them with blue tarp. Then they put mattresses, sheets, and blankets underneath the makeshift facility. I asked Jonas what they were doing. He said they were building a recovery room. The men had made a field-grade ICU with only a machete. What did they know that we didn't? Tomorrow we would find out.

To think that all of this had been done without a Certificate of Need.

The warm glow of the setting sun spread over the sea. The latticework of sunlight and shadows danced around us as the sea breeze changed directions. It had been a long day.

Soon, Madame Madeline returned to prepare our dinner. She carried a large aluminum pot with handles on each side, a glass bowl, a gallon of Mazola oil, a long-handled spoon, and an iron grate measuring about eighteen inches square all in one trip. She fit the grate inside a stand that was twelve inches off the ground. After setting up, she placed a pink, kindergarten-sized chair with a cane seat in front of her stand. Her flexibility allowed her to squat and sit kitty-corner on it. There, she could sit comfortably and rest her elbows on her knees. She was in position to cook.

I told Madame Madeline that I would like to watch her cook. She looked up at me, her eyes softening and her lips giving me a slight smile that said, "Watch this." She placed charcoal on the grate and lit it. The embers were glowing. It reminded me of making s'mores in Boy Scouts or on a college woodsy or over the family firepit. She poured an inch or so of the oil into the pot and set it on the coals. She then reached into a bag and pulled out freshly cut slivers of potatoes. She placed one layer into the hot oil. Using her spoon, she gently stirred them and ladled oil on top until they were golden brown. Then she transferred them to the glass bowl and repeated the process until she had fried them all. Once finished, she salted the mound of fries and covered them with tinfoil. I gave her a thumbs up.

Madame Madeline nodded in recognition before returning to her grocery bag. This time, she procured a package of hot dogs. She sliced them crosswise on an angle, sautéed them, wrapped them in tinfoil, and set them aside. Finally, she pulled out spaghetti noodles, which she cooked in the same pot. She mixed the noodles and the meat in a large serving bowl and set it on the table next to the plastic plates and stainless cutlery. A bottle of ketchup on the side of the table would be the sauce.

Our Italian gourmet meal a la Madame Madeline was ready. Crisp, golden fries, al dente pasta, and hot dog marinara made in one pot with one utensil had never tasted so good. Madame Madeline won Top Chef.

CHAPTER 16

Out in the Countryside

After dinner, I walked toward the cove to watch the sun cast its last rays across the tranquil sea. A five-star resort could not have provided finer cuisine, a better view, or better service. As I looked out into the sea, I noticed a lone fisherman standing at the back of his canoe, deftly paddling out for a catch. Maybe tomorrow, Madeline could sauté or fry fresh fish. But, for now, I tried to enjoy the scene in front of me. It had been a long day, and the cool sea breeze offered hope of a long and restful sleep.

Once I returned from my walk, Tom, Bob, Bill, and I headed for the dorm hallway and took the door to the left. The women in our group, meanwhile, went through the door on the right. It did not take long for us to unpack and hit the sack. Lying on my back and looking through the springs of the top bunk, I saw the local night vermin scurrying across the rafters. Fortunately, we had no snacks for them. During the night, there were minor tremors that caused the beds to sway just a bit. We reassured Tom and Bob, who were spending their first night in post-earthquake Haiti, that this was common. Once the tremors passed, I focused on the sounds outside; mangoes dropped to the sandy soil and sounded like golf balls landing on the green.

I slept soundly until my full bladder required attention. It was 6 a.m. and pitch black.

I was sitting on the edge of my bed, adjusting my eyesight, when everything began to shake. It felt just like the 4.3 quake I had experienced on La Gonâve. I looked up at the steel rafters, and they were holding. If something were to fall, the empty upper bunk would be protective. It seemed there was no need to panic. I was about to stand up and go outside to the latrine when Bob, awakened by the tremor, jolted out of his bed on the opposite side of the room. He covered the back of his head and bolted toward the door, bent over like a fullback charging into the end zone. The door was closed. He smashed into it head-on and at full speed, bounced back three feet, and landed spread-eagled at the foot of my bed. He was stuffed at the goal line.

The noise woke everyone up. Bob sat up—and then stood up so that he could hold onto the bed frame. We sighed a breath of relief as we realized that he was all right. Surgeons can be impulsive and hardheaded sometimes. Having heard the noise, the women across the hall knocked on our door and asked if everyone was okay. By now, we were laughing and kidding him. For some reason, the women felt that we were being insensitive during a stressful situation.

After this tumultuous beginning, the morning turned calm, with oatmeal, mango, and coffee for breakfast. Suddenly, we heard a sharp whistle up by the front gate. A Haitian Boy Scout troop, dressed in crisply pressed uniforms, marched in formation towards us. As they got closer, we saw that they were carrying the Haitian flag and regulation army stretchers. I had no idea how they had gotten here, why they had come, or how much we would need their services. When they reached the place where we were standing, we directed them to place the stretchers against the wall. They stood at attention and waited for further instructions.

After greeting the Boy Scout troop, we got to work. We had, by this time, established our centers of excellence. Wound cleaning would be done in chairs or on the bottom bunks in the yard. The fracture assessment and casting would be done on blankets on the ground. Operations would be done on folding tables, with disposable sterile drapes covering them. The fracture and wound debridement cases were fairly routine by now. It was the surgical ones that would be stunning.

A girl of about ten walked in with her parents. A red-and-white-checked cloth covered her nose and mouth. The girl looked like a bandit in an old Western movie. Her eyes gazed at each of us, showing a mixture of hope and apprehension. We had her sit down. Her mother removed the bandana, revealing a layer of gauze wrapped around her head and mouth. After she carefully removed the bandage, I understood the mixed messages from her eyes of hope and apprehension.

A pie-shaped wedge of flesh was missing from her face. The apex was at her right nostril. One jagged edge sliced to the right corner of her upper lip; the other went to the center. The exposed flesh was full of crusted blood and weeping serum. Fortunately, her gums and teeth were intact. Nevertheless, the site was like a giant, raw cleft lip. We would not be able to close this wound at our makeshift facility. This sweet patient needed a flap or skin graft—and possibly multiple procedures. All we could do for now was clean and redress her wound.

We checked with Roger, who told us that one of the hospitals in Port-au-Prince had reopened and was being staffed by trauma surgeons and orthopedists. We asked him to check if any plastic surgeons were available. Jonas told the family what we were doing and that they should wait until we had more information. Several hours later, Roger learned that a plastic surgeon was due to arrive at the hospital tomorrow or the next day. We gave them more gauze and antibiotic ointment to use until she could see a surgeon. Jonas instructed the family on how to keep the wound clean until she could have it repaired appropriately.

Now we just needed to transport the girl and her family to the hospital. A young man standing nearby offered to take the girl and her mother to the hospital. He mounted his motorcycle. He had the girl sit in front of him, while he instructed her mother to sit behind him on whatever remained of the seat. Perfectly balanced, like a high wire team, they headed out the gate. Her dad said he would catch up later.

We got back to work. Next, another dad or uncle walked up. His left arm, bent at the elbow across his chest, provided a seat for a three-year-old girl. Resting her head on his shoulder, she held onto his shirt collar with her left hand. Her face and left arm showed no signs of injury. Her white dress was clean. She looked as if she were going to church, not this makeshift trauma center. Jonas asked how we could help. With a slow, gentle twist of his arm, the man rotated the girl away from his chest and gingerly brought her right arm out from its hiding place.

It was then that we saw that strips of torn shirts had been wrapped around her hand, forming a ball the size of a naval orange. Dr. Bob unraveled the layers. None were blood-soaked, and they peeled off easily. Finally, the last one was removed. We saw no cut, gouge, or loss of skin. Her thumb and index finger were normal. However, the middle finger, ring finger, and little finger were swollen and blacker than her skin. When he touched her fingers, he could feel a bubbly sensation underneath the skin. It was crepitus, the result of gas produced by bacteria.

Our collective nausea was palpable. Gangrene. It was something that old diabetics got in their toes, not something a healthy, innocent child got on her hand. But poor circulation because of a crush injury can be just as devastating as vascular disease from high blood sugar. Her condition required that we treat it immediately. Further delay could result in more extensive involvement, sepsis, and possible death. Dr. Kate explained all of this to the man. He said okay and gave the girl to Kate to hold. As he sat on a chair a few feet from the operating table, he cradled his head in his giant hands and stared at the ground.

Bob placed the girl on the operating table. One of the volunteer nurses placed her hands on the girl's shoulders to comfort her. Leaning in next to her left ear, she sang songs just above a whisper. The music was a tonic for all of us. Bob examined her more carefully, numbed the hand with Novocain, and started the amputation. For the next two hours, he was extremely meticulous, removing dead tissues until he found healthy ones at the first knuckles. Throughout the procedure, the girl remained perfectly still and even seemed to be asleep at times. Maybe it was the music. Maybe it was innate stoicism. Maybe it was prayer. Or maybe it was all of the above.

In the end, she lost only three fingers. Her dainty thumb and first finger, although they now looked like a crab claw, had survived and were functional. After her hand was wrapped in its new bandage, it looked the same as it had when she had arrived. Only now, it was safe to go to the hospital for her follow-up. Bob lifted her from the table and placed her into the man's open arms. He gathered her onto his chest. Standing up, he bowed his head slightly and said, "Mesi, doctur." That was all Bob needed.

As the day progressed, camping tents were pitched. Pickup trucks and motorcycles were parked in a far corner, while the yard filled up with more and more patients. Tom organized the triage table, recorded a history of the complaints on a three-by-five card, and handed it to a Boy Scout. The Scouts escorted the patients to the appropriate stations and sometimes assisted us.

Two Scouts headed in my direction and transported a woman in her mid-twenties on one of their army-green canvas stretchers. The words "pelvic pain" were printed and underlined on the note that they gave me. Jonas asked her where she hurt. The woman pointed to her back and started to cry. Jonas instructed the boys to lift the stretcher to the level of a table and hold it steady while we transferred her over. After placing her on her stomach, we slid a pillow under her face. Her feet dangled over the end of the table. She was able to wiggle her toes but did not want to try to move her legs.

At that point, Alison had come over to help. We rolled the bottom of the woman's loose-fitting white dress up over her hips. Strips of green cloth were loosely taped across her lower back. We removed the makeshift bandage. The bandage had been covering a cut in the skin that extended across her entire lower back. We covered her entire backside with sterile drapes, leaving an opening that isolated the injury. Looking at the wound, I saw that the edges were weeping like a skinned knee. The raw tissue would be easy enough to clean with hydrogen peroxide, but we needed to clean it to its depth. Beginning at the skin and then going beneath it, there was little resistance as we spread the edges apart. The woman was not thin. As we neared the depth of the wound, the lack of resistance became obvious. The fascia and muscles had also been severed. We gently separated their edges and stared at her vertebrae. The iliac crest glistened like a half moon over the ocean. We did not need an MRI. There were no fractures.

I asked Alison, "Have you seen one of these before?"

"No, I specialize in femur fractures," she replied.

I consulted Tom, Bill, and Bob. We reached a consensus: irrigate thoroughly, debride any necrotic tissue, suture the layers, and transport her to the hospital. Next to the table on which she was resting, we set up a back table with saline, sutures, and a skin stapler. One of the Scouts, whom I had taught sterile techniques, was now our back-table techni- cian, opening suture packs and handing us sterile gauze as we requested them. Our serendipitous surgical team spent two hours cleaning the woman's raw tissue, suturing small bleeders, and closing each layer—as if we had done this a hundred times before. After we applied the final skin sta- ple, we securely taped a thick layer of gauze over the wound. With that done, we returned her to the stretcher.

The transport Scouts took the woman up to the gate, where a driver stood by his pickup truck that had a mat- tress in its bed. He offered to drive the woman to the hospital in Port-au-Prince and would not make any stops unless he found an international medical unit being established along the way. As he drove off, I continued to be amazed at the resiliency, empathy, concern, and generosity of the Haitian people. They cared not only for each other, but also for us. The Boy Scouts, who had arrived without request, had proved invaluable, in spite of my original skepticism. They deserved a merit badge that outranked all others.

The rest of the day seemed mundane, as we dealt with scrapes, bruises, gouges, and the surprising number of femur fractures.

Later in the day, a man who appeared to be about twenty-five and had no body fat walked up to us. He wore no shirt. Five strips of two-inch-wide, royal blue cloth were wrapped around his lower rib cage. Each piece of cloth was tied in a neat bow and had been stacked in a straight line along his right side. The pieces of cloth might have come from what used to be his shirt. The man looked more like a taped-up, game-day-ready NFL defensive back than an earthquake victim. He told us that cinderblocks had fallen on him and pinned him to the floor—but that he had been able to push and crawl free of the mess. Beneath the homemade corset, we found bruises and tender ribs. His lungs were clear. It was a relief to assure him that his injured ribs were, although sore, not cracked or dangerous to his well-being. Sometimes, relieving stress or anxiety is more therapeutic than a surgery or an antibiotic.

Another day neared its end. The evening was cool. As the sun disappeared and the sea breeze shifted, the shadows of the mango trees danced over several small charcoal fires scattered about the grounds, where families were cooking dinners. Madame Madeline upped the ante with a delicate whole white fish sautéed with onions and garlic that rested on a bed of rice, with French green beans on the side. Sweet, juicy mango slices cleansed the palate. She must have known my wish.

After dinner, I asked Jonas, "What was it like when the

earthquake happened?"

He got up from the picnic table and led me to the edge of the cove.

"When the ground shook and the noise rumbled, we ran out of our homes," he began. Pointing to the mountains across the road, he said, "The hills looked like they came alive. They were heaving and rolling towards us like a giant green wave. In despair, we ran to this open spot at the edge of the water. I felt the earth move under my feet. I didn't know if I was going to be tossed in the air or swallowed up by a crack in the ground." He then turned and faced the sea. "Next, the water rushed away from the shore. It traveled out about four hundred meters to that jetty of rocks. The ocean floor was exposed all the way. The rocks stopped the flow, creating a tall wall of water that started to move back towards us. I thought it might be a tsunami and ran back toward the mountain. I was scared."

He paused, and then asked, "Why does God punish Haiti?"

I tried to assure him that tectonic plates shifting had caused the quake, not God's wrath.

"Well, we heard that the United States set off a bomb underneath the water that caused it," he replied.

I told him, "I didn't think we had any reason to do that."

"You know what it was really like?" he replied. "It was like a giant dinosaur buried deep in the earth woke up and started running."

God, a bomb, a dinosaur? Another multiple choice. I preferred the dinosaur option.

CHAPTER 17

Heading Home

The next few days began to blend together. The dramatic appearance of fractures and flesh wounds slipped into routine. Our triage system, the Scouts, the translators, and the friends and families were well coordinated in the efforts to provide care. Our field hospital initiative was operating at maximum efficiency.

We soon learned that another group of physicians from the States was preparing to join us. As I anticipated their arrival, I began to think that it might be the appropriate time to go home. I would not be abandoning this effort without replacements. My partners had been taking my calls, and I needed to return to my own practice. My best option was to go to the US Embassy and join the masses being evacuated. I had seen the long lines and knew that the red tape involved might necessitate a night or two of sleeping on the embassy grounds. It would be a small inconvenience before boarding a transport plane and flying to a State Department-designated destination in Florida—and then heading home. Wherever in Florida it might be, I could use my credit card to finish the trip.

I began to realize I would miss the companionship of every-one—and especially the cuisine of Madame Madeline.

My moment of reflection was interrupted by a commotion at the gate. We saw a cloud of dust as a black, battered, pickup truck and a new, white SUV tore down the driveway. They stopped in front of our triage center. Once parked, a TV crew carrying cameras and microphones jumped out of the SUV. A man sitting in the truck bed got out, lifted a boy, and carried him to my empty station. The TV crew accompanying the family had come from CNBC. The boy, Mike, had just been found after being buried in a collapsed building for eight days. Hearing of our operation, the crew had brought him here. I thought about the woman in Port-au-Prince, climbing through the rubble looking for something or someone. I hope she was as successful.

We placed Mike on the exam table. He was nine—and he was alert. Jonas translated that Mike was experiencing no pain. I took a closer look at Mike. His eyes followed my finger side to side and up and down. His tongue was dry, his lungs were clear, his ribs were not sore, and his abdomen was soft. Other than being dehydrated and scraped up a bit, he was in fine shape. We called him "Miracle Mike." We sent him over to the post-op area for further observation. I wondered if his normal life of minimal food and water had been a factor in his survival. We got him a banana and some water. He asked Jonas to bring him a Coke instead.

The TV crew informed us that although several medical units were being set up, none were as operational as ours. Like a coach telling his players, "Good job!" and encouraging them to get back out there and do it again, it gave us a boost of energy.

Pastor Jacob informed us that the new volunteer physician team would arrive in the next day or two. The plane would be picking up a group of USAID executives for the return flight to Michigan and might have room for two of us. If we wanted to go, he needed to send our passport information to the pilot and to customs at the private airport before we would be allowed to board. I was faced with yet another to go or not to go situation. I decided that if there was room, I would like to be on that flight. Now, it was a matter of timing and transportation. I would have to see how it played out.

The next day, Pastor Jacob escorted a fellow pastor who was pushing his wife in a wheelchair to the front of the line. She wore a black straw hat with a short brim and an orange band around the crown, a white blouse, and a green-and-violet-striped skirt that covered her untied black shoes. The woman's hands were folded in her lap and clung to a damp handkerchief. Her moist eyes and pursed lips evoked a sense of stoic anxiety and agony. Her husband let go of the handles and pulled her skirt up. The hem rose like a theater curtain. It stopped at her knees. While the right leg was normal, the left leg was twice as big from foot to midcalf. The skin was tense, and there was crepitus. She needed to go the hospital, now.

Pastor Jacob agreed to transport the woman in his truck. We made her as comfortable as possible in the front seat. Pastor Jacob also informed us that the plane would be arriving today. He said that if we wanted to try to catch the flight home, we could go with him. Bill said he was ready to go. He lived in Grand Rapids, the return flight's destination. He said that I could stay with him until I was able to make further arrangements to get home, I said that I was ready to go, too.

When we were in medical school, we were given a traditional black leather doctor's bag like ones used in the old days while making house calls. It contained a stethoscope, an otoscope, an ophthalmoscope, a reflex hammer, and a tuning fork. It served me well in medical school, but had been of little use ever since. It was sitting at home on a shelf in my office. Instead, I had my black Swiss Army backpack. During all of my trips to Haiti, it had served that purpose far better than my black leather doctor's bag ever had. I emptied it of all the supplies, making sure to hold onto my passport, wallet, pair of tan cargo pants, and long-sleeved, blue button-down shirt. I gave an extra set of blue scrubs to Jonas. I sought out Madame Madeline, gave her a hug, and promised I would make her spaghetti.

The return trip to Port-au-Prince was much less strenuous, as we knew our vehicle was sound and was traveling on flat or uphill terrain most of the time. Along the way, we saw clinics set up by Doctors Without Borders and another set up by an Israeli medical team. Closer to town, roadside stands selling vegetables, charcoal, rice, and beans were operating again. Survival is a strong motivator.

When we reached Port-au-Prince, we saw that some of the debris had been cleared from the streets. As we approached the wall around the hospital, we saw that it had minor cracks. Soldiers guarded the gate with rifles at their sides and pistols in their holsters. Pastor Jacob negotiated our entrance. Our blue scrubs seemed to be a positive point of discussion once again. We were granted safe passage.

Inside the walls, we examined the facility. A concrete circle provided an orderly entrance and exit to the emergency door. The yard was filled with waiting patients and multiple centers for outpatient evaluation, and minor procedures were being performed. Outside, multiple generators were humming. Inside, authentic operating rooms were fully staffed and functioning twenty-four hours a day. In a lot of ways, the outdoor facility was just like ours. It made us feel good that we had been on par with their efforts—and we made sure to compliment them on their work.

We left the pastor's wife in the care of an orthopedic surgeon. We tried to check on the young girl with the lip and the woman with the back injuries, but visitations were not high on the priority list for the busy staff. In addition, Pastor Jacob had gotten a call that the flight was in range and that we needed to get to the airport as soon as possible. Private planes were required to depart as soon after their landing as possible because of the congestion on the tarmac. Normally, the trip to the airport would last about forty-five minutes, but traffic could be congested and slow. We needed to go.

Pastor Jacob had become adept at navigating the crowded streets, which were repopulated with vendors and motorcycles. Life was at last returning to the city. Within an hour, we approached the UN guards, who recognized Pastor Jacob. They admitted him through the gate and directed him to what seemed like his reserved parking space. We got out of the truck, walked to the familiar tarmac, and looked for our plane. We were ready to go back home.

The tarmac was full of planes and people. There were military cargo planes that looked like giant metal cornucopias unloading tons of shrink-wrapped supplies. Nearby, another crowd of Haitian men, women, and children hovered behind a police barrier, waiting anxiously with their backpacks, shopping bags, or purses in hand. They had been processed through the embassy and were waiting to board the evacuation plane. When the door opened, they moved en masse, like a swarm of bees, orderly and with a purpose. In about two hours, they would be in the States and making their way to stay with friends or relatives.

We saw our jet land, taxi, and park next to other small craft, away from the larger planes. We were careful to avoid other taxiing planes as we approached the side door of ours. When the door opened, the stair ramp extended out and down. One of the physicians, wearing full camo gear and hunting boots, descended, jumped off the bottom steps, and assumed a squatting, ninja-like pose. He then scoured the surroundings like a radar scanner. This was his first trip to Haiti, he told me. I assured him that there was no imminent danger and that he would be well cared for. Nevertheless, I still wanted to give him a Xanax.

Once all the people and supplies were unloaded, I introduced the new medical team to Pastor Jacob. I explained that he would be the Haitian boss man. I stressed that they needed to identify their boss man to ensure that all further activities would be most efficiently and safely accomplished. In general, physicians are trained to be independent and self-reliant, so I knew that this would be somewhat of a challenge. Here and now, they needed hierarchy to avoid anarchy. Fortunately, one of the doctors had been on a mission trip before and was selected.

It was getting late in the afternoon, and we were ready to board. The Gulfstream was well-equipped with soft, tan leather seats. In the galley, we could choose from a variety of deli sandwiches, chips, and a choice of sodas, bottled water, or iced tea. I chose chicken salad on a croissant and water. It was most refreshing. The meal seemed decadent but was appreciated.

We buckled up and took off. The ascent was smooth, steep, and quick. After we reached cruising altitude, the copilot came out of the cockpit and asked if anyone wanted to sit in his seat.

It was like I was a kid at the dime store with my grandfa-ther, listening to him tell me I could pick out anything and he would pay for it. I accepted the copilot's offer. The cockpit was overwhelming with its myriad of gauges, switches, and buttons. The only one I understood was autopilot.

I had never flown at 45,000 feet with a clear, 180-degree view of the world. It was absolutely breathtaking. As I looked to the left, I saw the sun low on the horizon. As I looked to the right, I saw a dark ridge high above the earth arcing from north to south. It seemed to approach us like a bank of slow-moving thunderstorms in the Midwest or a cloud of dark soil riding the wind during the dust bowls of the thir-ties. I asked the pilot if it was a storm front. He informed me that it's called the edge of night. Soon, it engulfed us like my grandmother's quilt covering me as she tucked into bed in her farmhouse attic. The transition to night was quiet, peaceful, and comforting.

The flight lasted only about four hours. When we were about to begin our descent, the copilot came in and told me that it was time for him to return to his post. I moved back to the cabin, reclined in the seat, and closed my eyes.

I was tired, but too revved up to sleep. There were so many divergent images and thoughts running through my mind, converging like two rivers creating turbulence, as they merged into one body of water: The devastation I had just left versus the luxury I now enjoyed. The bone-jarring truck rides in Haiti versus the smooth jet ride home. The open charcoal prepared meals versus the packaged sandwiches. The loss of family, friends, possessions, and records here versus the recent loss of retirement funds in the stock market crash two years before. The warm Caribbean days and cool nights ver-sus the sharp, cold January winds I was about to encounter.

It was a lot to think about and try to make sense of. How was I going to be able to explain any of it to anyone? How was I going to explain this road trip to someone who hadn't been there? It would take some time—and some writing.

CHAPTER 18

The Wedding

The black-tie wedding in the farmyard at the foothills of the
Rocky Mountains was a magnificent scene. Bales of hay covered with white tablecloths served as pews. The combination
of freshly cut grass mixed with the exquisite perfumes ema-
nating from the wrists and necks of the well-dressed women
provided a sophisticated, spalike aroma. The women had plastic guards for their high heels, while the men were allowed to
keep their Stetson hats on. The couple's chocolate Lab, carrying the rings in an antique jewelry box hanging from a Tiffany
blue ribbon beneath his neck served as the ring bearer for the
happy couple. As the dog strode up the aisle, he looked from
side to side, making sure that all eyes approved of his role.
He finished his walk and sat between the couple. The officiate extracted the rings from the jewelry box and proclaimed
the couple's union. Each held the other's face and exchanged
a tender kiss.

"Cheers, cheers! To the bride and groom!" everyone pro-claimed. The toast and symphonic clink of the crystal cham-pagne flutes rose into the thin Colorado air like a harmonized chorus of angels. It was a confirmation of the guests' support and a signal to proceed to the reception area, which was only a few steps away.

The food and beverage stations were an elaborate setup. White, peaked canopies shielded the stations from the sun and possible pop-up showers. Large portable fans set on low kept the air moving and the flying insets at bay. Votive candles and columbine flowers were interspersed between the platters of medium-rare filet of beef or bison, poached salmon garnished with sprigs of dill, shrimp on ice, and herb-crusted Colorado rack of lamb lollipops. Candied pecans, dried cranberries, and crumbled blue cheese seemed to play hide-and-seek among the crisp leaves of baby-bib lettuce. Grilled asparagus dusted with Parmigianino Reggiano and lemon zest sat beside bright green haricot verts supporting islands of toasted almond slivers. There were free-range chicken fingers, hot dogs, and Jell-O cubes for the children.

The open bar and the dance floor were at opposite ends of the area, separated by the tables and chairs, where everyone was eating. The disc jockey interspersed music for the two-step, line dancing, and the waltz. "Mustang Sally," "Brown-Eyed Girl," "The Way You Look Tonight," and" "Wonderful World" (the Willie Nelson rendition) were the crowd favor-ites—and the DJ appropriately responded with encores and requests.

After dining and dancing for a while, I wound my way the bar. It was stocked with Grey Goose vodka, Macallan scotch, a small batch of Colorado whiskey, Hendrick's gin, a variety of mixes and sodas, and a large, galvanized tub of Coors on ice. The wine selections included Whispering Angel Rose, Silver Oak Cabaret, Willamette Valley Pinot Noir, and Chalk Hill Sauvignon Blanc. Bottled water filled another tub. John Denver's "Rocky Mountain High" played in the background.

I found myself standing next to a gentleman in a tailored tuxedo. We both held a scotch on the rocks and toasted to the food, the company, and the future of the newlyweds. His nails bore the subtle buff of a recent manicure.

I said that the bride was my niece. He told me that he was the godfather of the groom, whose dad had recently died.

We exchanged the usual chitchat about sports, weather, current events, and the grandeur of the Rockies. Then, I asked what he did.

"I'm a financial adviser for a few select clients. Most of them athletes or entertainers."

I knew better than to ask whom. Instead, I asked what it was like to be involved in their lives.

"They are just like all of us," he began. "Some want to satisfy every spending impulse and need to be reigned in. Some want pile it up and just look at their accounts every day. Some want to diversify and plan for a future devoid of their talents or abilities. To outsiders, it may seem glamorous, but it is difficult work."

He was calm, confident, and comfortable in his own skin— not boastful.

"How about you? What do you do?"

"I'm a physician. An OB-GYN."

"I thought about being a doctor but couldn't get through organic chemistry."

"That's very common. It was a tough course for me."

"So what hobbies do you have?" he asked.

"Golf is a great diversion."

"Same for me, but all the travel I do for my clients makes it hard to find the time. Skiing, though, is more manageable, as my back door has access to the slopes in Aspen. Great family sport, too."

Once again, he seemed to be stating the facts, not bragging.

Then he asked, "Are you involved in any community activities?"

"Well, over the years, I've donated some time to the school board, church committees, soup kitchens, homeless shelters, and so on. A group of others and I have spent a lot of time developing projects in Haiti. How about you?"

"Same kind of things. I'm on the national board for United Way. Tell me more about Haiti."

I explained my trips—not only as they related to medical services, but also in terms of how the partnership had been instrumental in water purification projects, educational support, nutritional programs for children, and microfinance initiatives. As I spoke, I tempered my enthusiasm. In the past, I had overloaded a willing ear to a point where the response would be, "That's admirable," or, "I don't know how you do it," or, "It must be so rewarding"—and the discussion would soon end like a final flicker from a spent candle.

He took a sip of his drink and asked the bartender for a topper.

He said, "You know, I've thought about doing something like that."

At this point most people add, "But I need to wait until the children are grown or I'm closer to retirement or it seems safer there or I know there is something I could offer."

He didn't select any of the above. He waited for my response.

I offered him the opportunity to go with me on an exploratory trip. "It could be as short or as long as you want. It would be one of discernment."

He said, "I can't go."

"Why?" I asked.

"I am afraid of how it would change me," he replied.

I took a sip of my drink.

"You are correct; it will change you—and you might be the most honest man I've ever met."

We toasted, and I gave him my card.

"Let me know if you ever change your mind."

The disc jockey ended his set with "The Load Out and Stay" by Jackson Browne.

CHAPTER 19

The Dream

At 6 a.m., the alarm clock rang, and a transformer exploded in front of the house. The night had been full of thunderstorms, the driving rain interrupting a night off call. Darkness prevailed outside and inside. It was time to drag my reluctant body out of bed, shower, shave, dress, and go to the hospital to make rounds. Dressing in the dark was easy. I put on khaki pants, a blue, long-sleeved, button-down Oxford shirt, and a pair of cordovan penny loafers. This preppy outfit I had acquired in my college days remained an acceptable ensemble through all these years—and it hung on closet hooks, ever on the ready like a fireman's outfit. Ready to get going, I decided that I would just grab a coffee at the hospital.

The rain stopped. I left the house, went to the driveway, and unlocked the door of my thirteen-year-old red BMW 325 ix. I turned the key, but nothing happened. Great. A night spent without much sleep, then no electricity, and now a dead battery. What was next?

The hospital was only a few blocks away. Maybe the walk would do me good. Maybe the exercise would help my attitude. The challenge would be crossing Peachtree Street's six lanes. Although there was a stoplight at the corner, the consensus of drivers in Atlanta was that green means full speed ahead, yellow means gun it to get through the intersection, and red means get ready to slam on the brakes. Then, there were cars darting into open spaces of the lanes to the right or left, usually without using their turn signals. Another hazard was drivers making a sharp right or left turn, focusing on whether they could zip in front of the oncoming traffic without regard for any pedestrians.

I left home and trudged up the two blocks to the intersection. The traffic light was out. The drivers were not stopping, and only a few slowed down. It was even more dramatic to watch one driver perform a lane toss. A lane toss happens when a car that is travelling full speed suddenly realizes there is a stopped vehicle in front of it. While slamming on the brakes is an option, the driver knows that that would likely result in a rear-end collision. Instead, one can choose to crank the steering wheel hard to the right or left, in the direction of whichever lane seems most open. The car will then pop over and avoid causing the wreck that would be your fault. Just as a forward pass in football has two bad outcomes (an interception or an incompletion) and one good outcome (a completion), the lane toss has two bad outcomes (hitting or sideswiping a car) and one good outcome (making a clean transition).

I was contemplating my crossing strategy when it began to drizzle. I didn't have an umbrella. When I turned to go back, I was startled by a man standing right behind me. The man wore a rumpled, grey pinstriped suit, a partially buttoned vest, a white, open-collared shirt, laced black shoes, and an

Atlanta Braves baseball cap. His scraggly, tightly curled beard was sparse but covered most of his face. His hands had swollen knuckles and split nails, but they appeared strong. His skin was the color of rich mahogany. I figured he was one of Atlanta's homeless and would be asking me for money to get a coffee and sausage biscuit at the nearby Wendy's.

It was always a debate of whether to give it or not. In my mind, it's always a question of whether it's best to give enough for a quick meal or refuse the request, justifying my action on the grounds that it will perpetuate this behavior. Ignoring or walking by a panhandler sitting on the sidewalk with a hat outstretched is easy. Stopping at a red light, sitting in my car with the windows closed and looking straight ahead when someone approaches is also easy. This encounter was personal and was a bit unsettling. I would not be able to just ignore this man.

"Needin' to cross the street?" he asked.

"Yes," I replied.

"Me, too. It's not easy under any circumstances. Even worse today, with no lights working, dark skies above, and havin' a dark skin. I blend into the darkness. People don't see me so well. Sometimes, it's like I don't exist. Sometimes, I surprise them, like I did with you. I've been brushed a few times, but never hit directly or given any permanent injuries. Never know what's coming next. Gotta stay alert. People are in such a hurry. Don't seem to care about anyone but himself or herself. Sometimes, I think, I'll just wait for things to die down before I make a move. Sometimes, I think, someone will see me and pay attention. Sometimes, I think, if I just wait, my time will come. But it hasn't."

When is he going to ask me for the money?

"Want to try it together?" he asked.

"Uh, sure," I answered.

"The way I see it, you are white and more easily seen by others. But I have seen things you haven't seen. I can anticipate potential problems. And together we might make it."

"Uh, okay."

We stepped off the curb and moved to the edge of the first lane. Baby steps.

He began to explain the procedure to me. "First thing you need to know is that we got to take one lane at a time. Look too far ahead, you can be blindsided. If you want to know where a car is headed, look at the front tire. It is the first thing to change direction. Look at the fender or hood, it's too late. Next, you need to hold your arms out for balance and perception, like whiskers on a cat."

And so it began. I followed his lead. We bent forward or backward; we leaned left or right. We hopped, stopped, and tapped a few hoods, fenders, and trunks as we navigated the mobile maze. Though yelling at the drivers did no essential good, we yelled anyway: "Watch out!" "What are you doin'?" "Slow down!" "Pay attention, jerk!" "Give us a break, a--hole." On occasion, someone slowed, and we could hold a hand upright and say, "Thank you."

After a few seconds that seemed like hours, we crossed two lanes. After the third lane, we were halfway across. We stood side by side for a minute and changed our focus from avoiding the traffic coming from the left to avoiding the cars that were coming at us from the right. Then, we found a rhythm. Like a basketball fast break or a running back moving with his blockers, it seemed as if we were gliding in slow motion and with ease. It was like a runner's high. We were in the zone. The opposite curb, our destination, was now in sight. The second half seemed as if we had made the trip in no time at all. Oh,

fickle time, you can stretch forever or be gone in a nanosec-
ond. It's all perception.

Once we raced across the curb and onto the grassy knoll
of Ted's Montana Grill, my breathing was quick and shallow,
like a panting dog. I bent over and let the adrenaline rush sub-
side. My clothes were still clean. The stranger stood next to
me, took in a slow, deep breath through his nostrils, held it
for a count of seven, and exhaled through his mouth with a
slight grunt. He seemed to be recovering much quicker than
me with some sort of yoga technique.

"Thanks for the help," I began. "That was exhausting. I'm
on the way to the hospital. I have a lot to do today." Surely now
he's going to ask for money, I thought to myself.

But instead, the stranger turned to leave. Maybe it was my
turn to question him.

I asked, "Hey, where are you going? What are you going to
do? Are you okay?"

He turned back, faced me, and put his left hand on my
right shoulder. With his right hand curled into a fist, he gave
me a gentle jab directly over my heart.

"I'll be okay. You go on," is all he said.

I watched him head towards downtown.

"Hey, what's your name?" I yelled.

"Walter, Walter F. Man, Walter Free Man. My friends call
me Morgan."

At 6 a.m., the alarm rang. The sunlight was bursting
through the second-floor French doors that opened onto a
small terrace, where chives, sage, parsley, thyme, and lavender
grew in terracotta pots. I rubbed the deep sleep from my eyes
and got out of bed. I had been dreaming. The alarm had shattered the dream into a thousand scattered pieces. The images
were so vivid, the actions so real, the conversations so clear,

but now all that clarity and meaning had become vague with the intrusion of reality. I needed to try to retrieve, reassemble, and analyze them before I went to work.

What was that all about? What did Walter represent? Was it the poor? Was it his race? Haiti? Did it mean any one of them would be okay without me? Was it my dark side? Did it mean I had met my dark side? Did it mean I could accept my dark side? Did it mean I needed my dark side? Was it freedom? What kind of freedom? And what about Peachtree? Was it just a street, or was it a transition in life? What did the storm represent? What did the traffic light being out represent? What did the traffic represent? What about the fist bump on the chest? Was it just a friendly tap, or a pericardial thump meant to jump-start me, or a symbolic sledgehammer designed to break down protective layers? Was Walter an angel of sorts, or even God? So many questions, and surely more would come. It will take some time to answer them all.

It is impossible to know everything. We are mere mortals. We cannot control it all. It takes a measure of faith to trust that God has a plan.

Maybe it's another road trip.